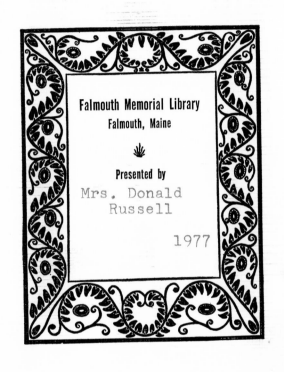

PERIOD NEEDLEPOINT
FOR ANTIQUE FURNITURE

Four Seasons Salon, Château of Breteuil (Yvelines).
This salon is decorated with paneling from the period of Louis XV. Its name derives from four magnificent tapestries very probably woven in a royal manufactury at the beginning of the eighteenth century. It is furnished with an outstanding suite in gilded wood, signed by P. Bernard, consisting of an ottoman, two easy chairs, eight armchairs covered in needlepoint and a screen. In the medallions are subjects taken from Aesop's *Fables*. They are set against backgrounds with sprays of roses, honeysuckle, and other flowers, rendered very naturalistically. (Plate "Plaisir de France")

PERIOD NEEDLEPOINT
FOR ANTIQUE FURNITURE

by Madeleine Jarry & Maryvonne Dobry

Translated by Phyllis Freeman

William Morrow & Company, Inc. New York 1976

Library of Congress Catalog Card Number 76-428

ISBN 0-688-03062-9

746.442

CONTENTS

A SELECTION OF DESIGNS FOR CHAIRS EXPLAINED AND DESIGNED BY MARYVONNE DOBRY

Preface

A great deal has been written about the history of furniture and especially about the history of chairs. No one, however, has written a book on the fabrics to use on chairs and how to use them in keeping with the style of the period. In short, there has been very little recognition of the importance of upholstery in the total effect made by an old chair or armchair.

Our purpose is to fill this gap, at least in part, through a study of chair coverings, specifically those executed in needlepoint. This book is designed to be practical; it is intended for all those who like to do needlework and who wish to stitch their own pieces for the period chairs in their homes. We want to help them to achieve this goal while also avoiding errors in style.

The first part of this book places needlepoint for furniture in its historical context, recalling that many kings and queens were devoted to needlepoint as a pastime. Next there is a study of the technique of needlepoint, its materials and varieties of stitches. The final section presents about twenty designs of different periods, with the patterns diagramed and explained.

Needlepoint on canvas and woven tapestry are both made by hand, but the techniques are different and the resulting effects are very different as well. In woven tapestry (either high or low warp), it is the weft thread (of wool or silk) in the shuttle that creates the decoration as it crosses the warp, which it covers completely. The result looks something like the horizontally corded fabric known as rep. In a work done by needlepoint (which in France is often called *tapisserie au point*), it is the canvas that serves as the support for the wool or silk thread that is stitched to produce the design. Needlepoint is actually a form of embroidery, and it is capable of providing widely varying textures, depending on the stitches used.

Originally, the word *canvas* (deriving from the Old French *chenevas* and in turn from the Latin *cannabis*) designated a hempen cloth from which sheets and dish cloths were made. Today, "canvas" is applied to the open-weave fabric that is the basic support on which needlepoint is stitched.

The beginnings of needlepoint are very ancient and largely obscure. In France, few examples survive from before the sixteenth century, so for the study of this art we must resort to written documents—contemporary inventories, descriptions of the period, and the like. One difficulty is that very often no distinction is made between needlepoint and other kinds of embroidery. Even toward the end of the eighteenth century, in 1769, Saint-Aubin, the king's designer, wrote in *L'Art du Brodeur (The Art of the Embroiderer):* "One embroiders in the round, in low relief, in shades of gold, in satin stitch, in Scotch stitch, in *guipure,* in pieced work, with couching, in waffle stitch, in padded satin stitch, with *paillettes,* in buttonhole stitch, with jet, with silk, with chenille, with wool, in tapestry stitch, in chain stitch, in Marseilles, in knotted stitch, and in white." Such a range of stitches gives an idea of the importance of embroidery and of its role in dress and in furnishings. It is interesting to consider some of the sumptuous works executed for kings and great lords. Under the Ancien Régime, the court set the fashion. Furniture styles were created on the initiative of royalty, and the nobility and then the bourgeoisie took their inspiration from these models.

The popularity of tapestry for furniture was at its peak in the eighteenth century. Numerous orders for sets of chairs done in tapestry were commissioned from the factories of Beauvais, Aubusson, and even the Gobelins. But needlework stitched on canvas is unquestionably more captivating; the fabric that results is more alive, more colorful, and especially, more responsive to light than the too-regular surface produced by skillful tapestry weavers.

M. J.

HISTORY OF NEEDLEWORK

by Madeleine Jarry

A famous needlewoman, Catherine de Medici

The sedentary life in *châteaux* in the Middle Ages, and for some families until the seventeenth century, accounts for the important place that needlework occupied in society; ladies old and young devoted their entire attention to it. And kings, queens, wealthy lords, and powerful bishops employed embroiderers as a regular part of their household staffs. Their works were considered to be paintings done with needles, and designs for needlework (known as *cartons,* or cartoons) were commissioned from the most celebrated artists. The Duomo Museum in Florence possesses one of these remarkable embroideries whose designs were provided by Pollaiuolo. Until the last century, embroidery played a major role in dress and furnishings.

As to chairs in particular, as late as the sixteenth century, there was little variety in their shapes. Then an importation from Italy, a chair with a back and armrests—"the chair with arms," which is the ancestor of the present armchair—made its appearance in France and elsewhere in Western Europe. It consisted of a simple wooden framework supported by cross rails that carried the seat and connected the legs. The reinforcing stretchers below were adorned with one or two carved bands. The seat and the back, which was broader than it was high, were made of a sheet of stiff, embossed leather, dotted with big gilded nails. Armchairs were also made in an Italian style that resembled scissors (they were known as X chairs, Savonarolas, curule chairs, or simply as folding stools), and there were also *caquetoires* (gossip chairs), which had high narrow backs and trapezoidal seats.

At the French court, the most widely used seat was the *carreau,* a kind of hassock or voluminous cushion with a large silk tassel by which it was carried. *Carreaux* were placed on chairs or directly on the floor. "The custom at court is that when the queen is there, one sits only on the floor," wrote the Abbé de Brantôme, a sharp-witted observer of the manners of the times. Catherine de Medici's inventory records no fewer than 381 hassocks in a single chest. Some were made of tapestry, others were embroidered in gold and silver on silk or cloth of gold. Specialists provided the designs. And Catherine summoned to her court, from as far as Venice, Vinciolo, whose reputation for embroidery designs had spread throughout Europe. According to Brantôme, despite Catherine's political intrigues, she found time to do embroidery and needlepoint. All the women of the court were set to the work, including Catherine's daughters, Claude, Elisabeth, and Marguerite, along with their cousins the Guises and frequently Mary Stuart, the banished queen of Scotland. Queen Catherine "passed the time after dinner in laboring over her works in silk, in which she is as accomplished as it is possible to be."

Flowers for needlework: "His Majesty's Garden"

As far back as the sixteenth century, thanks to advances in printing, books of patterns or designs appeared throughout Europe. In 1527, in Cologne, Pierre Quinty published his "new and refined book on the art and science of embroidery, cutwork, tapestry, as well as other crafts that are done with the needle." Numerous artists published designs for ornaments, which met with immediate success. They were intended for various kinds of craftsmen—not only embroiderers and tapestry makers, but goldsmiths, glassmakers, seamstresses, stoneworkers, and "other people of intelligence."

Designers were always in search of something original with which to enliven their flower patterns. Outstanding among them was Jean Vallet, embroiderer by appointment to Henri IV. He explained his quest to the horticulturist Jean Robin, who created a garden and greenhouses for Vallet in which Robin grew all kinds of foreign plants little known in France at that time. He brought exotic flowers (the tulip among others) from distant lands, and he painstakingly cultivated them in a small enclosure. These efforts won him the title of "His Majesty's Botanist."

In 1608, at the urging of the ladies of the court, Vallet published an album of etchings of about a hundred rare plants under the title *Jardin du Roi très chrestien (Garden of His Most Christian Majesty).* From then on, many albums of this kind for embroidery made their appearance. Robin's horticultural grounds were purchased by Henri IV, and "His Majesty's Garden" became one of the dependencies of the Crown. In 1626, the physician and botanist Guy de la Brosse suggested that the plants could be used also in teaching medical students without interfering with the designers of embroidery and tapestry. This led to the creation of the first Botanical Garden and its Museum of Natural History.

Spurred by this innovation in Paris, Gaston d'Orléans, Louis XIII's brother, installed a garden of rare plants at Blois. He attracted celebrated artists to it and amassed a collection of 6,000 miniatures of flowers to serve as models for designs. After the prince's death, in 1660, the portfolios representing his plants, birds, animals, and *ménagerie,* painted by Nicolas Robert, were bought for Louis XIV by Colbert, the powerful minister whose achievements also included the establishment of the Academy of Sciences and the naming of Robert as painter of the king's apartments. It is worth noting that needlework was instrumental in the founding of one of the first collections of natural-history specimens in France, along with its better-known domestic and aesthetic contributions.

The Hungarian stitch

Contemporary inventories are the major source of documentation for antique needlepoint for chairs. Actually, although needlepoint is more durable than woven fabric, most of it that once covered chairs has worn out in the course of time, and there are few examples from before the seventeenth century. Those rare pieces that have survived have often been restored.

A great number of needlepoint stitches are employed in making coverings for furniture. As early as the Middle Ages, work of this kind was so common that the word *point* (meaning stitches of all kinds) became synonymous with needlepoint. Henry Havard, the author of the *Dictionnaire de l'ameublement (Dictionary of Furniture)*—a monumental opus published from 1887 to 1890—discovered in the Royal Inventory of Jewels drawn up at the château of Vincennes in 1418 a reference to "a little pouche embroidered in needlepoint" *(broderie à poins)*. In the sixteenth century, different kinds of stitches began to be classified. An inventory of furnishings brought from Pau to Nérac by order of the king of Navarre in 1578 mentions pieces of embroidered upholstery done in "the queen's stitch." In the curious little play entitled "La Chambrière à louer" (The Chambermaid for Hire), the heroine, boasting of her skills, proclaims:

> "I know petit point by heart
> Gros point and the Hungarian stitch
> For hassocks and upholstery."

The inventories distinguished between petit point and gros point. In fact, most often they were careful to specify the kind of stitch because the value of the cloth varied according to its difficulty and the time needed to execute it. Certainly gros point worked on coarse canvas, using several threads at once, required very much less time and also less skill than petit point, in which only a single thread was used to stitch a very fine canvas.

The Hungarian stitch, which we have just mentioned, was particularly popular during the whole of the seventeenth century. At that time, it designated a series of chevrons in which different colors were played off against each other. Numerous inventories recorded chairs covered with needlepoint in the Hungarian stitch and beds whose curtains were embellished with Hungarian stitch. In *The Miser,* Molière had a valet describe Harpagon's bedroom furnishings: "First, a four-poster bed, with bands of Hungarian stitch appliquéd very elegantly on olive-colored iloth, with six chairs and a quilt of the same, the whole in very good condition and lined in iridescent red and blue taffeta."

Until the eighteenth century, Hungarian stitch was so popular that cabinetmakers borrowed the name from needleworkers. On November 26, the furniture dealer Lazare Duvaux sold the duchess of Mortemart a chest of drawers "in oak with a satin-finished veneer in Hungarian stitch."

It is very likely Hungarian stitch, called also "zigzag embroidery" (in the Fouquet Inventory, 1661), that gave birth to the "Chinese stitch," which, rather than forming sharp chevrons, produces a wavy background. Giving this the name Chinese stitch is a manifestation of the intense infatuation with exoticism in this period.

Louis XIII chairs

There is a decidedly severe look about the Louis XIII chair, and because of its nearly vertical back, it is as uncomfortable as it looks. One of the most widespread characteristics of this style is the use of turnings (in the spiral, spool, bun-foot, and other distinctive shapes) on the legs, armposts, and the stretchers between the legs. As early as the second half of the seventeenth century, hassocks, cushions, and portable chair coverings were replaced by a covering that was fixed in place. This innovation—which originated in Italy—may not have made the chair very much softer, but it led to all the subsequent advances in comfort. Leather was most commonly used for the covering, but various fabrics were also employed: solid or patterned velvet, rich brocade, embroidered or appliquéd materials, and needlepoint. Next to geometric motifs, such as those done in the Hungarian stitch, the favorite designs were those that featured large flowers and fruits rendered naturalistically. For more than a century, from about 1570 to 1700, many of the chairs at the court, as well as in the homes of the nobility and the bourgeoisie, were like beds covered with a fabric fixed in place that entirely concealed the wooden frame, which was generally very crudely constructed. The Mazarin Inventory noted "three covers for armchairs, each made of 11 pieces done in flat stitch, two of them serving as seats and backs and the others to cover the wood of the armchair completely..."

In the seventeenth century, upholstery fabric was one of the most valued components of household furnishings. A chair was prized much less for its wood, its basic construction, than for the material that covered it. In inventories, what is called an upholstered bed includes not only the covers for the bed, for a table, and for chairs, but also the wall hangings, curtains, and screens—which were all designed as matching elements in a harmonious whole, Some chairs were bordered, in imitation of the beds and tables, with a kind of skirt or valance made of four bands of cloth that reached the ground.

The most complicated tales, hunts, allegories, landscapes, or reproductions of actual pictures and prints— nothing daunted the ladies of this period. They used petit point for entire beds and immense hangings. They were extremely knowledgeable about the resources of this kind of work, and skilled at utilizing them. Sometimes they used gold and silver threads in their gros point and petit point. Sometimes, instead of stitching the whole area of the work, they cut out a small piece and appliquéd it on silk, velvet, or wool in the form of florets, bouquets, and edging. An inventory of the château of Chenonceaux in 1603 recorded "twelve pieces of embroidery in silk, adorned with gold and silver in gros point on canvas, to serve as a border for small rugs." Still another inventory, of the château of Nancy, dated 1608, cites "a hassock of crimson satin, on which are a hen and her chicks worked in cross stitch in gold, silver, and colored silk."

Armchair in carved, gilded wood. Régence period. Royal Ontario Museum.
This sumptuous chair is covered in petit point of wool, silk, and metallic threads, in the basketweave stitch. It depicts mythological scenes from Aesop's *Fables*.

Embroidery workshops under Louis XIV

We know that Louis XIV had several personal embroiderers who were employed solely in fashioning adornments for his clothing. And he also relied on the Gobelins Manufactury, which was not devoted exclusively to weaving tapestry. Charles Lebrun, the king's painter, had assembled there a number of craftsmen of all kinds to work on royal furnishings. Simon Fayette and Philibert Balland directed embroidery workshops there; some of their craftsmen were engaged in embroidering hangings, curtains, and fabric for furniture for the palace of Versailles.

In addition the convents of Saint Joseph and Saint Cyr were famous for the needlewomen at their workshop. In 1641 the Saint Joseph community settled in Paris, on the rue Saint-Dominique, and there "a number of young women were taken and taught to work on projects suitable for their age and sex." Among their projects was supplying magnificent furnishings for Versailles, for instance, the work "in blue velvet embellished with gold embroidery" that Madame de Montespan had made for his highness the dauphin, at Versailles, in 1668. She also had the Saint Joseph needlewomen make several pieces "for this prince's porcelain room": two large armchairs, twelve stools, and a bench, all covered in "petit point, with a brown background adorned with gold and enriched with silver and blue." After her fall from grace, Madame de Montespan withdrew in 1681 to this community, which she had supported with her favor in the past. The Metropolitan Museum in New York and the Bank of France in Paris still have some of the magnificent draperies in needlepoint on canvas executed in this convent after original designs by Lebrun; they depict the "Seasons" and the "Elements," with the faces of the children of Louis XIV and Madame de Montespan.

Ill. p. 13

In 1683, the château of Noisy at Saint Cyr was restored through the efforts of Louis XIV, and on February 3, 1684 Madame de Maintenon arranged for women to be brought there to teach young ladies religion, the French language, mathematics, a little history and music, and especially needlework. There Madame de Maintenon installed one of the foremost embroiderers of Paris, Lherminot, with three or four needlewomen, under whose tutelage the students became expert enough to embroider a handsome bed for the king.

In the countryside, there were other noteworthy religious communities that in some towns had excellent needlewomen—the Ursulines, Carmelites, the Nuns of the Visitation.

As in earlier centuries, some artists spent much of their time making patterns intended not only for embroidery and needlepoint but also for woven fabrics, jewelry, and goldwork. Abraham Bosse provided a set of forty drawings of plants for the king's sitting room. Striking flower designs were also created by the celebrated painter of the Gobelins Manufactury, Jean-Baptiste Monnoyer, and his pupil, Jean Vauquer, a skilled engraver from Blois. The style of decoration was dominated by the work of Paul Androuet du Cerceau, until the end of the century, when Jean Bérain the elder, who designed the king's bedroom and sitting room, devised a new style with graceful arabesques and fantastic ornamentation.

Ill. p. 15

Many chairs covered in needlepoint have survived from the second half of the seventeenth century. Their typical design consists of large flowers, often poppies, and plump fruits rendered with a realism that is thoroughly French. These brightly colored areas are juxtaposed with strongly marked lights and shadows and a few half tones, which cover the entire background. Gradually, these motifs became symmetrical: a bouquet of various

Seette with sides, in carved walnut. Régence period. Private collection.
This needlepoint on canvas displays a basket of flowers and fruits (grapes and watermelons are prominent) on the back and the seat, and poppies on either side. The design spreads out so exuberantly that the background can scarcely be seen.

flowers (roses, carnations, peonies) in a vase or basket is set on a lighter background that in turn is surrounded by scrolled foliage that forms a kind of frame.

A second kind of needlepoint contains a central cartouche depicting a fable, a mythological, rustic, or "Chinese" scene—the last a harbinger of the vogue of exoticism. (At Versailles, the duke of Burgundy responded to this trend by presenting the princess, his wife, with "a Chinese casket containing everything useful to people who like to do needlepoint.")

The "narrative" element in these tapestries is placed on a contrasting counterbackground somewhat darker than the background itself, and worked in larger stitches. Its ornamental motifs consist of leafy scrollwork,

15

arabesques, and more or less geometric lines. Under Bérain's influence, the design became lighter, the compositions less crowded, and shells, feathers, masks, and other small ornaments made their appearance. Needlepoint was universally popular, and letters and memoirs teem with allusions to it. Contemporaries reported that Madame de Maintenon—like the royal princess—was an enthusiastic needleworker. Here is one description: "Scarcely was she settled in her coach, and even before the driver had set his whip to the horses, when she took up her spectacles and pulled out the work she had in her bag." According to Saint-Simon, she read and worked on her needlepoint every evening while the king deliberated with his ministers. Saint-Simon also relates that the marquis of Vervins spent several years in bed, occupying himself with needlepoint. Madame de Sévigné, confined to her estate at Les Rochers, passed her time in working "two strips of needlepoint" given her by Madame de Caraman. In 1675, she wrote her daughter to send her yarn and a canvas, as well as "a pattern on which to work."

As in our day, these ladies did not always have the patience to finish their work. They hired women from outside their households to come to their aid, and in Antoine Furetière's *Dictionnaire universel,* published in the seventeenth century, the entry for the word "needlepointer" reads: "This is a maid whom one engages to do needlepoint and who usually works by the day."

The riches of the Sun King's furniture storerooms

The Louis XIV style is unmistakably the style of a king, and the armchair of his era marvelously expresses the feeling of grandeur. Built for men who wanted to increase their height (they wore wigs with curls piled high and high heels), the Louis XIV chair has a very high back and a seat wide enough for two. All its ample and luxuriously ornamented forms exude an aura of nobility. In this period, armchairs (the term now entered the language instead of "chair with arms"), chairs with a back, stools, and benches had molded and carved legs, sometimes in the shape of a baluster, sometimes like a quiver, very often like a bracket. Their feet resembled flattened balls or claws. The cross stretcher, in an H or X shape, was indispensable since the chairs were so massive and heavy that their base would be pushed outward and come apart if it was not securely braced at the bottom. Armrests usually were twisted into a massive crook adorned with carved acanthus leaves. The chairs were covered in tapestry and needlepoint, as well as brocade, velvet, and damask. The splendid trimmings were often completed by a long silk or woolen fringe that went around the seat and was overlaid with gold or silver embroidery.

Needlework in gold, silver, and silk was the most highly prized, and it was often used to depict "stories" on covers for chairs and beds, as well as on wall hangings. The Inventory of Crown Furniture for 1673 mentioned "a petit point hanging embellished with gold and silk representing the fables of Ovid's *Metamorphoses,* in three pieces, each composed of an octagonal picture in the middle and the device of the Salamander in each of the four corners."

The splendor of these stitched furniture coverings is evoked vividly in the account the journal *Le Mercure* gave of the visit in 1686 of the ambassadors from Siam to the royal furniture storerooms: "They saw sixty beds of supreme magnificence, for one did not want to show them those that are less beautiful, although they too are very sumptuous. The first ones that they viewed came from Persia, Turkey, China, Portugal, and several other nations where the finest work is done.

There is the coronation bed, with embroidery on two sides that is estimated to be worth 600,000 livres; the bed with the story of Proserpina, and the so-called bed of Queen Marguerite; there are beds done in petit point; those who see them at a distance of four steps take the petit point for a painting; and there are others on backgrounds of gold and on backgrounds of silver, others embroidered on velvets of all colors...''

The new eighteenth-century art of living

The Louis XIV style waned in the last years of the seventeenth century, and the Régence style began well before the regency itself was established, in 1715. While the sovereign grew old at Versailles, artists and artisans worked for others. Their clientele consisted of cultivated, wealthy, and idle aristocrats, who had the time to become deeply involved in the novel task of arranging the interiors of their homes. Because of these particular circumstances early in the eighteenth century, the golden age of French furniture had its beginning. This society was self-indulgent, and its chairs are above all comfortable; the legs are shortened, the backs curve in to fit the shape of the body better. One can dream, stretch out, even sleep, in these downy easy chairs. The chaises longues, the *duchesses* (daybeds or two-part chaises longues), the *veilleuses* (couches with a rest for the head and arm at one end) were created for weary ladies who had "the vapors."

What identifies a Régence or Louis XV chair immediately is its curved lines—especially the S curve of its legs. The back posts and the front seat rails in particular have strongly marked scrolled profiles. The armrests are shaped like brackets and are placed slightly behind the legs in order to allow women wearing dresses with panniers to sit down easily. The back of the chair is lowered. When it is flat, it is called "à la reine" ("in the style of the queen"). Around 1740 a chair with a concave, enveloping back, the cabriole chair, was developed. Chairs now reveal their wooden structure, most frequently carved and molded. They were made by carpenters joined in a single guild with cabinetmakers known as *ébénistes* (ebony workers, from *ébène,* "ebony"). They continued the medieval tradition, working in the same way and using tools very similar to those of the past. They lived in the section of Paris where their ancestors had settled, a little west of the Porte Saint-Denis, chiefly in the rue de Cléry and rue de Bourbon, the present rue d'Aboukir.

A decree promulgated in 1743 required each carpenter and cabinetmarker to brand his personal stamp on the furniture that came from his workshop. This measure, designed to maintain the quality of workmanship, was not immediately or always applied so that it is not unusual to find beautiful furniture of the time that does not bear the stamp.

During the entire eighteenth century, the term "furniture" meant generally a set of chairs: armchairs, side chairs, easy chairs, along with a settee or sofa and possibly a firescreen and folding screen. The Four Seasons Frontispiece Salon of the château of Breteuil, hung with very beautiful tapestries, is furnished with chairs signed P. Bernard. The group, in gilded wood, includes an ottoman, two easy chairs, eight armchairs, and a screen. They are covered with an extremely clear, lively needlepoint. The subjects in the central medallions are drawn from Aesop's *Fables,* and the backgrounds are embellished with ravishing flowers—roses, honeysuckle, cornflowers—rendered very naturalistically.

Armchair à la reine, in carved beech, painted and gilded.
Louis XV period. Musée des Arts Décoratifs, Paris.
This armchair, richly carved with flowers, foliage, and other rococo details, still retains its original paint and needlepoint upholstery, as well as its original webbing. On the back and seat is an asymmetrical spray of exotic flowers bursting from a scrolled rock.

18

Armchair à la reine, in painted beech with molding and carving. Louis XV period, stamped J. B. Cresson. Musée des Arts Décoratifs, Paris.
Chinese motifs worked in *camaïeu*—three shades of blue on a light background—make up this handsome needlepoint covering. The central motif is framed by a garland of flowers and scrolled rocks that echo the contours of the wooden frame.

Armchair in carved beech. Régence period.
Private collection.
This large, very low armchair is supported by short cambered legs, ending in sockets. The caned back is covered with a cushion made, like the covering for the rest of the chair, in needlepoint. The design is worked in a *camaïeu* or monochrome, here consisting of three shades of green on a light background. Exotic stylized fruits and flowers are symmetrically arranged.

Ill. p. 18

Ill. p. 19

Ill. p. 21

Ill. p. 23

Around 1730 the *rocaille* (literally, "rockwork") style came into being, made fashionable by ornamental artists such as Pineau, Oppenordt, Slodtz, and Meissonnier. *Rocaille* chairs have asymmetrical twining carvings, and a jagged shell is the dominant motif. The Musée des Arts Décoratifs in Paris has a beautiful armchair, with a large design and rich carving of flowers, foliage, and scrolled shells. It is very excehtional in still having its original webbing. In addition, it retains its original polychrome paint and needlepoint covering, with exotic flowers and foliage designed especially for this chair.

Another noteworthy armchair à la reine from the Musée des Arts Décoratifs is stamped J. B. Cresson and has *rocailles* and acanthus leaves carved on it. It is covered in needlepoint in three shades of blue, which stands out against the background of a natural color matched to the paint on the wood. This design is inspired by the *chinoiserie* in vogue in the eighteenth century.

Attention to detail and refinement are sometimes pushed to the extreme, as evidenced by the chair in the Musée du Louvre signed Tilliard. It is covered in needlepoint whose colors harmonize with the green and gold lacquering of the wood.

Flowers, depicted very naturalistically, continue to be the principal source of inspiration. In relation to the preceding period, the proportion of decorative details is reduced, and the backgrounds are less crowded; artfully composed bouquets are arranged in pleasing and graceful undulations. Other examples show veritable little pictures, country scenes, sheaves of musical instruments, and especially La Fontaine's *Fables* with numerous animals set against a background bordered with flowers.

Chair à la reine, in wood painted green and gold, Louis XV period, stamped Tilliard. Musée du Louvre. In this extremely elegant chair, the line of the back, which tends to "break down" in the lower part, presages the end of the Louis XV style. The design on the back shows a musician surrounded by animals and plants. The color scheme of the needlepoint was chosen to harmonize with the paint on the wood.

In the eighteenth century, at the Gobelins Manufactury, the Savonnerie, and especially Beauvais and Aubusson, many tapestries for chairs were woven on looms. It was at Beauvais that for the first time tapestries were woven based on La Fontaine's *Fables,* after the designs by J. B. Oudry, manager of the factory. These cartoons were woven repeatedly in the other tapestry workshops of the region. Along with the celebrated Oudry; Boucher, Leprince, Pillement, Tessier, and Jacques also painted cartoons. They were designed for weaving, but they inspired needlepoint works as well.

In the middle of the eighteenth century, by extension, woven tapestries began to be called petit point or gros point, depending on their fineness. This is an erroneous usage, since tapestries are woven with a shuttle and therefore do not involve stitches. However, in the sale of Madame de Pompadour's furniture, March 27, 1765, there is mention of "a piece of furniture from Gobelins, in petit point, not mounted in its full beauty." Today the application of the term petit point to Gobelins or Aubusson has become common usage.

A royal pastime

In 1769, the designer to the king, Rivet, known as Germain de Saint-Aubin, published his book on the art of the embroiderer. This book, whose importance for our subject we have mentioned earlier (p. 8), provides numerous designs for needlework, among them ornaments containing interlaced initials made of eglantines and morning glories. Saint-Aubin also gives us a picture of the legal status of his colleagues: "There were eight independent embroiderers chartered in the community and solely under the jurisdiction of the military guard of the palace; they bore the title of 'embroiderer to the king by royal warrant.' In addition, there were two embroiderers privately charged with the work for the crown. These embroiderers to the king had the right, when very pressed in their undertakings, to have the guard carry off by force the workers who suited them from the masters' houses."

At court, embroidery always enjoyed great popularity, and it remains the pastime of women of the nobility. One is reminded of this by the "terrible quarrel" between Louis XV and his favorite, the countess de Mailly, reported by the marquis d'Argenson, foreign minister to the king. It erupted January 17, 1741, according to d'Argenson's *Mémoires:* "Everybody has acquired a taste for needlepoint. Madame de Mailly herself is busy with it; she was so absorbed in it that she did not respond at all to the king when he addressed a question to her. At last the king, thoroughly provoked, threatened her, and then, taking a knife from his pocket, he slashed the needlepoint into four pieces..." A frightful row ensued!

On the other side, the duke de Luynes informs us about the activities of the queen: "Several days ago, the queen presented Madame de Luynes with a piece of needlepoint worked with gold, which is in part her own handiwork..."

The queen's entire entourage followed her example. There was no diversion that the king's four daughters cherished more than doing this kind of work. Madame Campan, Marie Antoinette's secretary, wrote in her *Mémoires:* "The ladies of the court, returning home, undid their waistbands and took up their needlepoint and I my book." Louis XV himself was infected with the "passion" for needlepoint. D'Argenson wrote: "The king has suddenly started to do needlepoint. This decision was so unexpected that it took a masterstroke by a courtier to satisfy it so swiftly. Recourse was had to Monsieur de Gesvres, whose chief occupation is just that. The

Cabriole armchair in polished beech with moldings. Louis XVI period.
Collection Brocard.
The upholstery of needlepoint on canvas is in the transition style between Louis XV and Louis XVI. Branches of tea roses are scattered over a crimson background.

Child's sofa, in molded and carved wood painted gray. Louis XVI period, stamped Pluvinet. Private collection. The needlepoint on the seat and on the back shows a graceful bouquet of roses arranged symmetrically and tied with a ribbon. Delicate beribboned leaves form a frame for both pieces.

Chair in gilded wood. Louis XVI period, stamped J. B. Sené. Chantilly, Musée Condé.

The concave cabriole back terminates at the top in a basket handle curve, framed by two small columns. It is covered in a tapestry made at the royal manufactury at Beauvais. At the center of the seat and of the back is a bouquet of flowers on a creamy-pink background, surrounded by a very graceful garland of flowers and leaves following the design of the wood. The seat is furnished with a wide tapestry band *(plate-bande)* ornamented with flowers and fruits which goes around it entirely.

courier who went from Versailles to Paris to fetch what was needed—a frame, yarn, needles—took only two and a quarter hours in going and returning; this is something that will very much enhance the credit of M. de Gesvres..."

If we can trust the duke de Luynes, it was at Marly that the Bien-Aimé, the beloved and widely loving king, was taken with this whim, and on the subsequent trip he made to La Muette, his hunting lodge, there were already seven or eight frames being used by the most eminent lords of the court. Before long the provinces copied Paris. As for the ladies, until the end of the Ancien Régime, they remained faithful to their needlepoint. "At Trianon, even when Marie Antoinette entered her drawing room, her women did not leave their needlepoint frames,"

Madame Campan wrote, and added later: "There is still in existence in Paris, at the home of Mlle. Dubuquois, a needleworker, a carpet made by the queen and by Madame Elisabeth [sister of Marie Antoinette's husband, Louis XVI] for the large room in her apartment on the ground floor of the Tuileries. The Empress Josephine saw and admired this carpet, and directed that it be preserved in the hope that it might reach Madame one day."

Return to antiquity: Louis XVI chairs

The return to antiquity, as early as the middle of the eighteenth century, indicates the beginning of a new style. One of the great transformations in furniture that marks the passage from the Louis XV to the Louis XVI style is the change in the line of the legs from cambered to straight.

The straight legs were most often of turned wood that was ornamented with fine groovings, either straight or in spirals. A master such as Georges Jacob created numerous varieties in shape and design. The Louis XVI chair is characterized by its straight lines and geometric appearance; the back is oval (flat or in the concave cabriole shape), square, or rectangular. The seat itself is most frequently trapezoidal. The over-all effect is rather cold; even its very fine carving, when gilded, resembles chiseled metal.

In the area of designs for fabric and needlepoint upholstery for chairs, the Louis XVI style meant the return to a classical order and symmetry. There are vertical, widely spaced stripes strewn with small floral decorations Ill. p. 111 such as rosebuds, flowering branches, or miniature bouquets. There are countless lyrical and rustic appurtenances set inside squares or medallions: baskets of various kinds, ribbons, country hats, flutes, pipes, Ill. p. 103 tambourines, shepherd's crooks. The bouquets of beribboned flowers in the style of J. B. Huet and Ranson were accompanied with arabesques that became increasingly attenuated. On a chair upholstery was often finished off with a *plate-bande* (a wide vertical band) decorated with flowers that went entirely around it.

The discovery of the frescoes at Pompeii influenced design considerably. Chairs were upholstered in needlepoint that depicted ancient ewers, musical instruments, mythological figures—all in a simulated antique style. These ornaments stood out in a monochromatic *camaïeu* against the darker background of a medallion bordered with beading and surrounded with flowers and ribbons in delicate colors.

Needlepoint on canvas continued to enjoy great favor until the end of the Ancien Régime. The newspaper *L'Avant-Coureur* for March 12, 1770, for instance, informs us that "M. Dubuquois, tapestry merchant by appointment to his grace the dauphin, is showing this year, in his shop on the rue Saint-Honoré, petit point done for armchairs, cabrioles, side chairs, easy chairs, sofas, ottomans, etc.... He also creates designs for ladies who wish to do this kind of work themselves."

The nineteenth century

As soon as the regime of the Directoire (1795-99) had somewhat restored the elegance swept away in 1789 by the Revolution, embroidery reappeared, but it was now for the most part embroidery for dresses and formal costumes; embroidered motifs of Greek-key patterns and garlands of laurel were intended to recall classical vestments.

Mahogany chair, Empire period, stamped Jacob Desmalter. Private collection.

The double-pear turnings of the front feet are characteristic of this style, but the reverse-curve back has an unusually fine openwork grill at its base. The seat and back are covered with needlepoint consisting of a repeat-pattern background with a caning effect against which a rosette is placed inside an octagonal frame. At each corner there is the Empire palmette.

The furniture of the Empire period, which followed the Directoire, was vast in its proportions. The rear legs of chairs, usually in the back-curving saber shape, are widely spaced to provide a sturdy base; the front legs are carved into scabbards, quivers, or pilasters, ornamented with carved palmettes. Their upper parts end in a female bust or a sphinx head; their feet terminate in a lion's paw or an inverted palmette. In other designs, the feet have a single or double pear shape, or even two overlapping balusters. The backs are usually rectilinear, but they also display the gondola shape, with its enveloping concave curve. The success of this new contour, which lasted for the twenty years from the Directoire to the Restoration of the monarchy, is explained by the fact that high waists were in style in ladies' clothing.

Ill. p. 26
Ill. p. 63
To cover the luxurious chairs of the imperial palace, sumptuous silks made in Lyons were used. Napoleon wished to revive industry in Lyons, and as early as 1804 he sent orders to the factories there. From their threads, the Beauvais and Aubusson workshops wove tapestries for chairs in a variety of designs: palms, laurel wreaths, stars, foliage, and bees. Lahameyade de Saint-Ange dominated designing for the whole first half of the century, creating countless projects. In needlepoint for chairs, flowers give way to mythological scenes and emblems of the empire.

Ill. p. 27
With the restoration of the Bourbon kings, the taste for needlepoint revived. Charming designs of bouquets of flowers were created for chairs in light woods (burl ash, burl elm, maple, lemon wood), made fashionable by the Duchess de Berry. She was a dedicated needlepointer, and in the château of Sully, at Rosny, there is still furniture

Armchair in burl ash with amaranth marquetry. Restoration period, stamped Werner. Collection J. Chélo.

The ocher background of this needlepoint was chosen to harmonize with the warm tone of the burl ash of the chair frame. Light woods—ash, elm, maple—reached their peak of popularity in the early nineteenth-century Restoration era, supplanting mahogany, which had been favored during the Empire period. A large bouquet in a romantic style blooms on the back and seat, and even the *plate-bande* is decorated.

covered with the needlepoint she made with the help of her ladies-in-waiting. And we know that in his last years, the doughty General Cambronne, celebrated for his courage at Waterloo, became an ardent needlepointer.

The romantic period gave a new popularity to this kind of work. This was true not only in France but also in the rest of Europe, especially in Germany and Austria, and it remained in favor until the end of the nineteenth century. In order to cover chairs of hybrid shapes inspired by the Louis XV style, or even more by that of Louis
Ill. p. 119
Ill. p. 29
XVI — "the empress style" — ladies stitched a variety of designs: large bouquets of flowers in bloom, birds, Chinese themes, geometric designs in very vivid and often harsh colors.

Chairs now became the creation of upholsterers rather than of cabinetmakers. They covered the body with fabric and placed a fringe around the base that covered the legs. Around 1825 the elastic spring, fashioned of flexible iron wire, was invented by the upholsterer Chare. This brought an end to the manufacture of hard chairs that required soft cushions. Some years later, in 1838, another manufacturer conceived the notion of padded chairs, without any wood visible. Countless varieties of these extremely comfortable chairs were created: low armchairs *(crapauds, bébés)*, love seats, divans, small sofas, and especially the *pouf*, a puffy cushion that serves as a large stool. Broad bands worked in needlepoint with brilliantly colored yarns were appliquéed on the fabrics that covered these chairs.

Near the Palais Royal, on the rue Batave, the firm of Picot was established to specialize in embroidery for the sovereigns of the nineteenth century. This enterprise was bought in 1880 by Robert Brocard. The *Journal des Dames (Ladies' Journal)* and the *Magasin des Demoiselles (Young Ladies' Magazine)*, which had dominated their audience in the early part of the century, were supplanted in 1851 by the *Guide Sajou*, which styled itself the "Only complete journal of Ladies' work : Knitting, Embroidery, Lace, Needlepoint, Crochet, Tatting, etc." It offered colored designs in gouache—ranging from morning glories, rosebuds, Pompadour medallions, and garlands of vine leaves, to birds of paradise and even a white greyhound bitch! Other designs were entirely geometric. All the colors were vivid and in strong contrast, set against a very dark background. Toward the end of the century, Thérèse de Dillmont wrote her *Encyclopédie des ouvrages de dames* (published in English as *The Encyclopedia of Needlework*). It was enormously successful, and has remained to our day one of the best introductions to needlework.

Doing needlepoint today

After an eclipse of a dozen years or so, needlepoint in France has again become popular. Who among us has not been tempted to stitch a needlepoint covering for a small Louis XV cabriole or a pad for a Directoire chair? We have seen that needlepoint has been pursued in the distant past and in the noblest circles. Queens of France have preceded us in this adventure. But what to choose, how to begin? The designs offered in shops are very inexpensive, but they are not always appropriate for period furniture. To commission a design from firms that specialize in such work is very often prohibitively expensive. That is why Maryvonne Dobry has selected these designs which she proposes that you work out with her.

Mahogany chair. Napoleon III period.
Collection Mme. G.-R.
This delicately colonnaded back is pierced at
the top by a hand grip. The needlepoint seat,
in wool and silk, with composite stitches in
gros point and Smyrna cross, is geometric in
design. Its lively colors contrast effectively
with the black edging.

THE ART OF NEEDLEPOINT

by Maryvonne Dobry

Needlepoint is done on canvas, which is covered completely in the course of the work. This is what distinguishes it from embroidery, in which some of the fabric backing is always allowed to show through. Needlepoint also differs from other kinds of needlework in not being exclusively "women's work." It is a very ancient tradition with many devotees of both sexes down through the ages.

Your participation in the entire needlepoint process from the beginning will greatly add to the joy of creation. Consequently, we guide you step by step, from identifying the style of your chair, to choosing the design, drawing it yourself, and carefully selecting the range of colors you will use. It is here that you can add personal touches in accord with your own individual taste.

In the matter of colors, you must visualize how the colors of the needlepoint will harmonize with the rest of the furnishings. There are simple or very ornate designs, monochromatic *camaïeux,* with one dominant color broken down into several tones, or rich polychromes to suit each style. Further, you must consider the effect you wish to create. A multicolored design with a busy pattern produces a slightly three-dimensional look, like a relief, and the background area seems to recede and shrink (which is desirable for large chairs). A piece worked in *camaïeu* "shrinks" less—depending also on the design.

You must not only follow your taste, but also take into consideration your own temperament. While to some it may seem tiresome to cover large surfaces with repeat patterns or make row after row of uniform stitches on a large solid background, for others this may be a means of relaxation. Some people love to work complicated designs, like a puzzle, and enjoy breaking each area of color down into several shades.

Because it is a characteristic of needlepoint that the stitches touch each other, the stiffness of the original drawing disappears in the course of the work. No line is ever hard—or curved—exactly. The softness and richness of the wool also modifies the designs, and each person's hand always reveals an individual intent. And with large stitches or fine stitches (gros point or petit point), a brilliant or a delicate palette—what a wealth of different possibilities needlepoint offers!

"Tapestry on canvas—or needlepoint—is very highly valued for furnishings, both to cover all kinds of chairs and cushions and to decorate valances and screens." This is the judgment of Larousse, the authoritative French dictionary. It is our purpose to show in detail the ideas to which Larousse refers.

In addition to the designs for chairs, you will find sections on background stitches and repeat patterns (pp. 56-61), which provide alternate approaches for covering period chairs. For Louis XIII, Louis XVI, and Empire chairs designs with repeat patterns are very appropriate.

If the size of your chairs makes you hesitate to undertake an endless work of covering back, seat, and arms, you can stitch some bands of period patterns (galons), which you can use in combination with velvet or silk upholstery. And you can also use strips of period patterns on the upholstery of large antique chairs or on the heavy but wonderfully comfortable turn-of-the century chairs.

Among the traditional eighteenth-century motifs you will find on the following pages are bouquets surrounded by foliage, baskets of flowers with arabesques of leaves or garlands—particularly for Louis XV or Louis XVI chairs—and the Chinese themes that were very much in vogue at that time.

You can give your imagination free rein in choosing needlepoint designs for piano stools or foot stools, round or rectangular stools, hassocks, benches, banquettes—provided, of course, that you keep within the proper period.

You can adapt our designs to make coverings for mantelpieces or tables (for low tables or stands, it may be wise to put a piece of protective glass over the needlepoint). For a folding screen or a firescreen of the Louis XV or Louis XVI period, you might take the central motif of one of our designs for chairs and place it inside a medallion (look at the period designs beginning on p. 71).

Pillows are essential to make a home comfortable, and it is difficult to have too many of them. You have a choice between covering them entirely with needlepoint or appliquéing small pieces of needlepoint on a solid backing of velvet or other fabric. All our designs are easily adapted to cushions, and you can readily devise a design by enlarging any particular detail that strikes your fancy.

MATERIALS AND EQUIPMENT

As is explained at greater length on pages 39-40, yarn colors for the designs in this book have been "translated" from the French Colbert and Médicis yarns used by the authors to comparable colors for Paternayan Persian yarn—which is the most readily available needlepoint yarn in the United States, as well as the one of the best quality and with the widest range of colors.

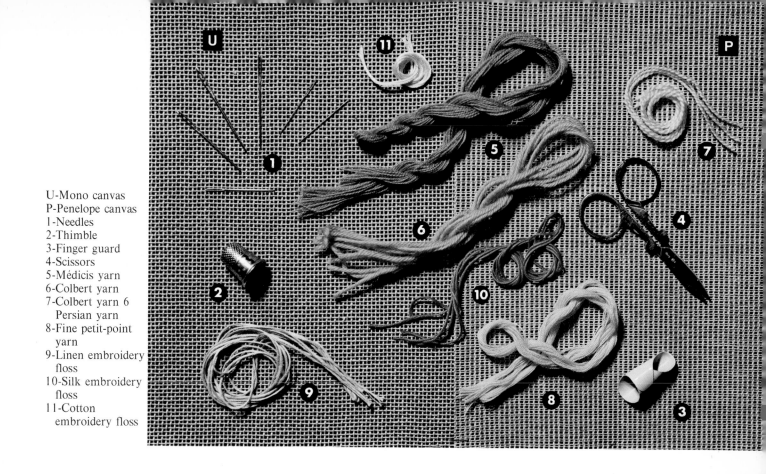

U-Mono canvas
P-Penelope canvas
1-Needles
2-Thimble
3-Finger guard
4-Scissors
5-Médicis yarn
6-Colbert yarn
7-Colbert yarn 6
 Persian yarn
8-Fine petit-point
 yarn
9-Linen embroidery
 floss
10-Silk embroidery
 floss
11-Cotton
 embroidery floss

However, the information on this and the following page concerning French needlepoint yarns is of interest. You may find some of them in exceptionally well-stocked needlepoint stores in this country and, in the future, the Colbert and Médicis yarns will probably become more available here through distribution by the famous old international firm of D.M.C.—a name already familiar to needleworkers who work with the D.M.C. cotton embroidery floss that is very widely distributed in America. *(Ed.)*

Mono canvas is a mesh of single threads of sized cotton. **Penolope** is a canvas woven of double threads, the 2 vertical (or warp) threads being closer together than the 2 horizontal (or weft) threads.

Canvas is the backing for all needlepoint, whether it is stitched in wool, silk, cotton, or a combination of them. Over the centuries, the nature of canvas has evolved considerably. In early times, plain canvas—used for coffee sacks, or burlap—was made from jute linen, and later, cotton. The Portuguese worked rugs on fishnet, and the Romantics, for whom no sentimental notion was too fantastic, stitched neckbands and bracelets on fine meshes of silk, horsehair, and even human hair!

Mono canvas, the only type known to the eighteenth century, which was the century when needlepoint reached its greatest heights, was especially well suited to the basketweave stitch. This stitch produces needlepoint with remarkable solidity and demands very close work.

Penolope did not appear until 1850, but it quickly became popular, since many people maintain that patterns show up better on it.

The coarseness of the canvas must be proportionate to the coarseness of the yarn (and vice versa). However, it is preferable not to choose the canvas until after you have identified the period of the chair to be covered, decided on the design and the stitch that suits it, and taken into consideration the experience and patience of the person who will work it. A novice should not choose a canvas that is too fine or a design that is too complicated; usually, it is difficult to do small sititches well, and small designs do not lend themselves to large stitches. In connection with the design, one should bear in mind that the principle of needlepoint is to make dovetailed stitches; curves are worked in steps, and the change from one color to the another is never defined by a sharp line.

Colbert yarn (number 6 in the photograph on the previous page) is a rather tightly twisted, 4-thread yarn and the one used by the authors of this book and by most French needlepointers. It comes in a large range of colors, 9 gradations per color, or about a thousand different shades in all.

Colbert yarn 6 (number 7 in the photograph) is the French Persian yarn, a close counterpart of the Persian yarns we are used to, a 3-thread strand loosely twisted. It is much easier to lift off a thread of this yarn than to lift threads from the 4-thread Colbert. The full 3-thread strand of Persian yarn is thicker than 4-thread Colbert.

Not shown in the photograph is a special type of yarn called *laine Spécial Fonds,* used for backgrounds, especially dark ones. It is thicker than 4-thread Colbert and therefore covers the canvas very uniformly. (Dark dyes tend to "crush" the yarn, making it actualy thinner than yarn dyed lighter shades, hence the fabrication of this special background yarn.)

Fine petit-point yarn called *laine Broder Figures* (number 8) is a beautiful fine yarn in a special range of colors for the stitching of tiny human figures in traditional designs.

Médicis yarn (number 5) is very fine, the classic French yarn which is stitched several strands at a time, even on a fine canvas. The range of colors is limited but handsome, all being subtle "antique" colors.

Linen embroidery floss (number 9) is used for backgrounds. It is best to choose a pale tone as the stronger ones tend to fade.

Silk embroidery floss, known as *Soie d'Alger* may be introduced to highlight and brighten almost any design, but it is rather fragile. (Silk backgrounds, very much in fashion in the past, have for the most part been abandoned because of this fragility.) However, it is often very successful to use silk to reembroider some of the yarn stitches: the center of a flower, stems, butterflies' antennas and legs, etc. But do not overdo the use of silk; remember that wool will last long after the silk has been pulverized by time. You may get a similar effect by using cotton embroidery floss (number 11), which has somewhat the sheen of silk.

It is very difficult to give a reliable gauge for the amount of yarn a given stitch will require on a given canvas worked by a given person. Some people work more tightly than others; some work unevenly; some people use the yarn to the very end; others leave long tails unworked. On the whole the best course is to make samples on a small piece of canvas, judge for yourself (the exercise will be useful when you come to work on the final canvas). A last note on equipment: some people like to use a thimble and/or a finger guard. The latter comes in two types—a rigid type and one of rubber that is designed to prevent scratching the needle. It is important to buy good needles for your work, neither too long nor too thick. English needles are the best. You will also need a pair of flat, small, sharp scissors. Embroidery scissors will not do; their fine-pointed blades easily catch on the threads of the canvas, rather than enabling you to snip at a single stitch of yarn.

Traditional standing frame
Napoleon III period
Collection M.D.

FRAMES

To prevent your needlepoint from getting out of shape and to keep your stitches perfectly aligned, it is best to work on a frame. There are several types, the classic one being **a floor or standing frame,** such as our grandmothers used. A wide range of frames is available, of greater and lesser elegance. (That may console you for not having come across one in your attic or at an antique shop.) To my mind, the simplest, in unvarnished fruitwood, are extremely charming.

The floor frame consists of a rectangular body that pivots on two supporting legs. Horizontal scroll rods at the top and bottom are furnished with nails or tapes on which you can tack the canvas. The space between the rollers is adjusted to the width of the canvas work area by means of long screw rods that form the vertical sides of the frame and are turned to keep the canvas taut.

When you stop working, you loosen the screws on the verticals slightly so that the canvas can "relax". You stitch with both hands, one above and one below, making two movements for each stitch: one to insert the needle into the canvas and the other to pull it through from below. There is no rule for the position of the hands, but it seems logical that the more deft hand be placed underneath, since it must blindly find the exact spot where the needle emerges. But in F.H. Drouais's beautiful portrait of Madame de Pompadour, she is embroidering—on a handsomely carved frame—and holding her *right* hand on top and the *left* underneath.

Table frames, which are smaller versions of the standing frame, come in several sizes. You place the table frame on the edge of a table or on your knees, and work above and below as with the large frame.

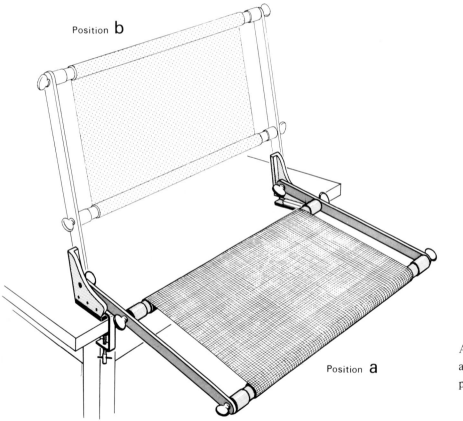

Position **b**

Position **a**

A new frame that can be easily set up and is suitable for fairly large needle-point.

It is clamped to the edge of a table, enabling you to work with both hands, as with the floor frame. On top, one rod holds the tacked canvas taut; another holds the canvas on the bottom. Adjustable screws regulate the length of canvas between the rods.

The **free frame,** which is also used in embroidery, is a compromise between working on the traditional frame and working without a frame. Like the table frame, its size is somewhat limited. And as on other frames, the canvas is attached to its adjustable edges with metal fasteners or strong thread.

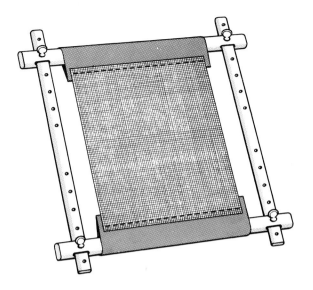

This frame can be rested against the edge of a table or against the back of a chair, and you can turn it upside down as you work. It combines the function of preventing the canvas from getting out of shape with the virtue of being completely portable.

If you want to make stitches in a single movement (the needle going in and out in one action) do not bend the work very much. And put your left index finger under the canvas. (The position of the finger is about the same as in sewing: it guides the needle.)

If your work is not very large and you want to take it with you to spend every single leisure moment on it, you must learn to do without the frame. If you take certain precautions, this is certainly feasible. Many people find that work goes more quickly without a frame because you then stitch as you sew, without dividing each stitch into two movements.

Using a weight instead of a frame

An alternative to the frame—one that can easily be arranged anywhere—is the method of using a weight to act as a kind of half-frame.

Begin by rolling the bottom of the canvas (right side out), keeping a firm hold on it. Rest the top on the edge of a table and hold it down with some kind of sturdy weight; this will keep it taut and prevent it from getting too much out of shape.

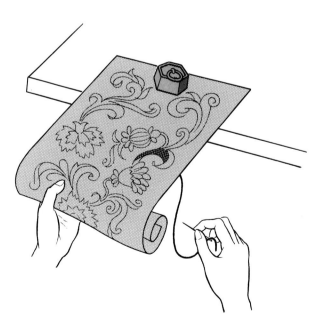

When you start to work, first stitch the motif in the middle and work downward. To work the other half, all you have to do is turn the canvas upside down. But be careful not to let any ridge show where the background stitches meet (see "Stitches"). This method can be used for cross stitch and Gobelin stitch.

For the half-cross stitch, you must be guided by the requirements of the "return" (see "Half-cross stitch"). For the basketweave stitch, do not use a weight until you have covered a fairly large vertical section of the work (see "Basketweave").

Working without a frame

If you work without a frame, you must keep the canvas rolled, right side out. This will prevent it from wrinkling, the design will stay sharp, the work clean, and everything will be firmly under control.

First roll the bottom. If you are doing the basketweave stitch, begin working at the top (first the design, then the background). After you have covered a fairly large section of the surface, also roll the canvas from the top. This will tighten the stitches already made instead of crushing them, and they will even out somewhat if they are irregular. The same applies to the Gobelin stitch. For the simple half-cross stitch and the cross stitch, you can work the canvas by halves, provided that you take care about the meeting points.

If the work is very large, put the top (already rolled) over the back of a chair to support it; it will hook on. To keep one or the other end of the canvas rolled to your convenience, tack the roll with a few loose stitches of wool.

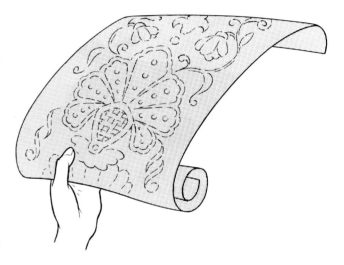

PERSIAN YARN COLORS

The authors of this book used for their designs primarily the French Colbert yarn shown as item number 6 in the color picture on page 33 plus the Médicis yarn shown as item number 5.

Item number 7 in the color picture is Colbert Persian yarn, called Colbert 6, which the authors do *not* use. It is a 3-thread strand closely resembling the Persian yarns we are accustomed to in the United States. Indeed, Colbert 6 is used by some needlepoint shops here to supplement their range of Persian colors. It can be used successfully on the same canvas with any other Persian yarn.

Many different kinds of needlepoint yarns, and so-called "tapestry" yarns, including imported yarns, are sold in this country. However, to make this book as simple and convenient as possible, for American needlepointers to use, we determined to use for the American edition just one yarn, and the one most widely available, Paternayan Persian yarn.

As mentioned before, this is the best needlepoint yarn produced in the United States and has the widest range of colors. Though the *gradations* of Paternayan colors are fewer than those supplied by Colbert (an average of 5 gradations to Colbert's 9), the actual number of Paternayan *colors* is greater than Colbert's range, which has a high percentage of muted "antique" tones. Persian yarn splits easily to 1 thread for petit point or you can add 1 thread to 1 strand for the coarser canvases. They are mothproofed, the dyes are remarkably fast against light, and the dye lots are dependably the same over the years.

In the French edition of their book, the authors specified colors of Colbert 4-thread yarn by the manufacturer's names and numbers. We have "translated" these to comparable Paternayan Persian colors. That is, we have compared the Colbert and Paternayan color-sample charts and have chosen for each Colbert color its nearest equivalent in Paternayan. Then we have given each color the simplest descriptive name possible (Paternayan only numbers and does not name its colors), to give you a mental picture of what you are trying to achieve. And then we have given the *number* of the Paternayan color; this is the number that your needlepoint shop uses to order Paternayan yarn from the wholesaler.

The result is that the lists of colors given with the designs in this book are highly specific. They were chosen from the full range of well over 300 numbered yarns on the Paternayan sample chart. However, no needlepoint shop can stock *all* the Paternayan colors made, particularly since some of the gradations of one color are very close together, and also because in many instances the variations from one basic color to the next are not very great. So, though our numbered lists are specific, they are intended only as a general guide, nevertheless. Most shops that buy Paternayan have a sample chart from which they order and from which you can get a clear idea of the general coloration intended by the authors. Then you must transpose to the colors actually available, and, rather than being bound rigidly to our original color list, work instead with the skeins of approximate equivalents, trying this combination and that, until you have before you a color scheme that is pleasing *in itself*.

If you do this and are flexible about your choices, you will arrive at something very good in any well-stocked shop. If you try always to get at the closest *number,* instead of using your own eyes and judgment, you will arrive at arbitrary combinations you will not be happy with. By all means get the help of experienced salespeople, but even so, do not settle for colors and combinations you do not like.

Remember, too, that colors in the skein are much brighter and contrast with each other more clearly than they will when they are stitched. (They also darken when they are stitched). Of course, for period furniture, a blast of violent color will not be appropriate. The authors' color choices are graceful blendings of color rather than Strong contrast. But they have not, except in one instance on page 127, where a faded antique tapestry on the back of an old chair was matched by a new needlepoint seat to replace the one that had worn out—they have not except in this instance used colors intended to look "faded." If you use some discretion in your choice of Paternayan colors, which are admittedly clearer than much of the Colbert range, you will create a piece that will become more gracefully muted with the passage of time.

Another point: If you particularly like the colors in a given color plate in this book, you would do best *not* to use the color list.

Though these plates are beautifully printed, it is a long distance from the original needlepoint, through the photographer's lighting, to the transparency, and on from there to color printing. The final color plate has inevitably departed from the original, which will mean that the specific color list and what you see in the plate will be subtly and confusingly different. To test the author's original and authentic intention, use the list. But if you want to match the color plate that pleases you, work directly with it and the real wools available to make your choices.

Finally, your shop can special-order colors for you. However, special orders for small quantities of yarn are difficult to come by. But for large background areas, the exact color may be very important to you, either because you are aiming for authenticity or perhaps covering a chair to work in a room with an established color scheme. Background colors in a design such as the one on page 23 is crucial. The amount of wool needed is considerable and should be no problem to special-order if necessary. *(Ed.)*

GETTING TO WORK

How to start and end a thread

First of all, do you know the proper way to thread your tapestry needle (as the needle for needlepoint is usually called)? Learn to do it rapidly and effortlessly. First, loop the end of a strand of yarn around the head of the needle. Do not take a long section of yarn; that will make it too thick. Bend only the end of the yarn; this is the thinnest part, so the strands will be fairly flat and slide readily through the eye of the needle. Grasp the folded yarn firmly between your thumb and index finger; then, carefully slide the needle out and bring the eye over the yarn, while you ease your grip a little. As the needle catches the end of the wool, gently push the looped yarn through the eye.

Although knots are forbidden in needlepoint, you are traditionally instructed to make one knot at the end of your yarn in order to start. Then insert the needle about an inch away from where you want to make the first stitch and pull it out at the desired place.
Work systematically, covering the end of the yarn on the wrong side with your first 6 or 7 stitches. Then let go of the needle, take the knot, pull it a little, and carefully cut the yarn flush with the canvas. The end will disappear. It is now caught on the back of the work and you do not have to worry about it any further (see the upper illustration).

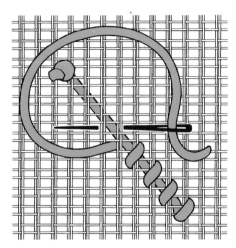

Use the opposite method when you come to the end of a strand: bring the end out a little (see the lower illustration), and hide it with 6 or 7 stitches on the wrong side, in the course of the following rows. (Be careful not to let it become thick.)

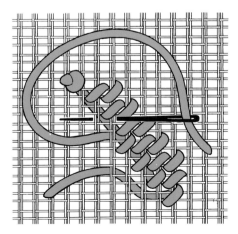

If you have a very flexible frame—or if you are working without a frame—you can turn the canvas on the wrong side. Then simply slip the end of the thread under the last stitches, pull it a little, and trim it flush. Be careful that you do not cut through any stitches or you risk having many of the threads come loose in the blocking.

THE STITCHES

It is not necessary to know all the needlepoint stitches in order to embark on a project that will be of real value in your home—and satisfying to you. If you are a novice, begin by making some practice stitches in half-cross stitch. This will help you familiarize yourself with the feel of the canvas and enable you to acquire some skill with the needle. Then you can quickly go on to more complicated stitches, and in no time you will end up letting yourself be tempted by the truly elaborate decorative stitches—those that needlepointers in bygone times embellished with gold and silver thread.

Simple half-cross stitch *(demi-point simple)*

The half-cross stitch is certainly the easiest needlepoint stitch. It is not the most solid, however. Consequently, its use is best confined to trimming cushions, firescreens, bell pulls, or other kinds of strips—in valances and borders of hangings. It is also suitable for small complicated motifs surrounded by larger areas of basketweave. The half-cross stitch is worked from left to right, horizontally, on penelope canvas, *never* on mono canvas.

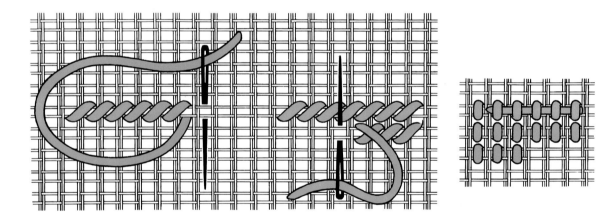

Going *(1st row)*: working from left to right, the needle is vertical; the stitch slants as it covers the intersection of the threads of the canvas (see the illustration at left). Since penelope is a 2-thread canvas, the intersection consists of 2 vertical threads of the canvas and 2 horizontal ones. **Return** *(2nd row)*: working from right to left, the needle remains vertical. You must avoid overloading the back of the work; there are two ways to prevent overloading: (a) For a few stitches: insert the needle from bottom to top (as in the center illustration). The stitches automatically fall under the stitches of the preceding row and slant in the same direction.
(b) For longer rows: turn the canvas upside down, which will place the next of row stitches in left to right position. (Check the stitches on the back of the canvas to see that they are parallel vertically.)

Half-cross stitch tramé (demi-point tramé)

This is an easy basic stitch that readily provides needlepoint with considerable body.

It is worked on penelope canvas only in two steps:

(a) First, tramé from right to left, inserting the needle between a pair of threads, over which you proceed to lay the yarn horizontally (study the diagram carefully).

(b) Second, work the half-cross stitch in the usual way—from left to right, the needle always vertical. With each stitch you will be crossing and covering the tramé thread.

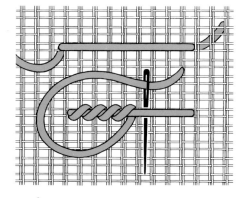

At the end of the row, to start the next row begin again to tramé from right to left; then work the half-cross stitch again from left to right, with all the stitches slanting evenly, one under the other.

You may wish to tramé beforehand. In that case, it is essential to use a frame.

If you are working on a large surface, you cannot run a single thread of yarn over the entire width. Stop every 6 or 8 stitches, insert the needle *under* the next pair of vertical threads, backstitch over them, and continue working again to the left. Make sure that the backstitched breaks do not fall in exactly the same vertical line. Following this method, you can also outline your colors with tramé. It will be necessary to split the yarn, to half the thickness of the yarn you are using for the final stitching. The yarn should be the color of the design to be filled in.

Cross stitch (point de croix)

As its name indicates, this stitch forms a cross. In contrast to the stamped cross-stitch work of our childhood, the *second* branch of the cross here must always slant to the right (as in the half-cross and basketweave stitches).

If you are working without a frame, your needle will go in and out of the canvas in one movement. You will then start working the first branch at the right:

Going: from right to left, with the needle vertical, your stitch slants toward the left as it covers the intersection of the vertical and horizontal threads of the canvas.

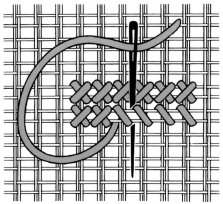

Return: proceeding from left to right, the needle still vertical, insert it into the same meshes of the canvas as you used in the first row. Because you are moving in the opposite direction, this stitch slants toward the right, and you will be forming a row of crosses.

Note: It is important to choose a firm quality of penelope canvas for this stitch, since the yarn must go into the same meshes 4 times.

Basketweave stitch (*point de Saint-Cyr*)

Madame de Maintenon gave this exquisite stitch a place of honor when she organized classes in needlework for the young ladies at the celebrated Saint Cyr school, which she founded with her protector, King Louis XIV. We commemorate this distinguished needlewoman by calling this stitch Saint Cyr. It is more widely known in English as the basketweave stitch. It is, in fact, identical with traditional petit point, except that the latter is always worked on very fine canvas.

Basketweave was particularly popular in the eighteenth century, which left us much beautiful furniture covered in needlepoint. The stitch may be worked on either mono canvas or penelope, but both more and less experienced needleworkers prefer to work it on mono canvas, and this is indeed the more authentic choice for period pieces, since it was the only canvas known to the eighteenth century.

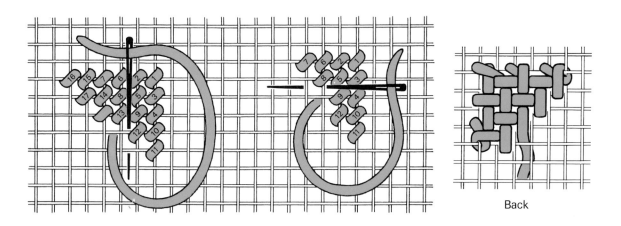

Back

One could almost say that this stitch is reversible: on the right side, the stitches all slant in the same direction, the stitches of each row dovetailing between the stitches of the previous row. On the back, the threads seem to be interlaced, as in a woven fabric. It is this aspect that gives rise to the name basketweave.

In basketweave, you work diagonally, beginning at the upper right of the canvas and finishing at the lower left. From right to left, the row moves upward; from left to right, it moves downward. The needle is horizontal when you go up; vertical when you go down.

Let us begin with a little exercise—making a square. Start at the upper right corner. In going up as well as down, you move in diagonal rows that are perpendicular on the front of the work to the slant of the stitches themselves.

One stitch, two stitches; on the third row, we should have 3 stitches (we are guided by a pencil line we have drawn in advance). It is essential to observe the position of the stitches carefully: on this third row, the needle is inserted between two stitches in the preceding row. This means that it is inserted in a mesh that is *already occupied*. It then goes under a stitch of the preceding row but comes out in an *unoccupied* mesh.

44

Summary

• From *left to right*, you go *down;* the needle is vertical. It is inserted between 2 stitches of the preceding row, in a mesh that is already occupied; it goes under 2 threads of mono canvas (or under 2 groups of 2 threads of penelope), and emerges exactly below a stitch in the preceding row.

• From *right to left*, you go *up;* the needle is horizontal. It is inserted between 2 stitches of the preceding row, in a mesh that is already occupied; it goes under 2 threads of mono canvas (or under 2 groups of 2 threads of penelope) of the preceding row, and emerges in an unused mesh.

The stitches must have a parallel slant and dovetail between each other. Be careful about the "dangerous turns" at the ends of rows. If you are following the vertical side of a square and turning to make an upward row, the first stitch of the new row will be placed directly under the last stitch of the row just finished, and the needle will be on a slant. Then, when you bring the needle back to the horizontal, you will automatically find the place to start the second stitch. Likewise, if you are following the horizontal side of a square and turning to make a downward row, the first stitch of the new row will be placed directly to the left of the last stitch of the row just finished, and the needle will again be on a slant to make it. Then, when you bring the needle back to the vertical, you will automatically find the place to start the second stitch.

If the motif or area has winding contours, in order to find the starting point, you must think carefully about where to put the first stitch of the new row so that its stitches will dovetail between those of the preceding row.

Note: Do not stop working at the end of a row if you can avoid it. Leave your needle in position for the next stitch so that when you pick it up again, you will be able to tell at once where to resume. If you have worked up to a point where a different color begins, and you must shift to another place in the canvas, you need only look at the back of the work to determine the direction in which to proceed; you must never disrupt the woven pattern of the back. If you are in doubt, before going on, try with your needle to determine whether you should be going up or down. The firmness and the neat finish of the basketweave stitch are due to the care you bring to it. Beginners sometimes find it difficult to work the motifs (especially if they are small) in basketweave. It is acceptable to do them in half-cross stitch on penelope canvas.

True petit point

Because of its fineness, petit point requires enormous patience, and it is generally used only for small areas—figures (an entire torso or faces and hands alone), florets or bowknots, butterflies or little birds. Sometimes it is known as quarter stitch *(quart de point),* referring to its minuscule size. It is worked diagonally, that is, in basketweave.

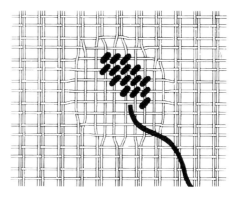

True petit point is far removed from the practice of inlaying a bit of very fine canvas in a mono canvas. Rather, you must use a piece of penelope and on it mark off the area to be worked in petit point. Wet the canvas and separate the threads very evenly to produce a fine grid (in the past a special comb was used for this purpose). The canvas will stiffen up as it dries. You then "paint with the needle" to create charming details.

Straight Gobelin stitch

This is called "Gobelin" stitch and not "Gobelins," since it is related only in appearance to the tapestry produced by the Gobelins Manufactury.

On mono canvas, it is worked by laying the strand of yarn over 2 vertical threads of the canvas. (If you wish, you may first tramé between the 2 horizontal threads of the canvas, which will then be covered by the stitches.) On penelope, the stitch is really spectacular. To work it, you hold the canvas the wrong way, that is, sideways (with the warp threads—the 2 closer threads—horizontal). You bring the yarn over both horizontal threads but *separate* or "split" the 2 vertical threads (study the illustrations carefully). While the stitches are being laid vertically on the front of the work, the needle slants slightly to the left (going) and to the right (return). If you look closely, you will see that the stitches form a slight herringbone on the back.

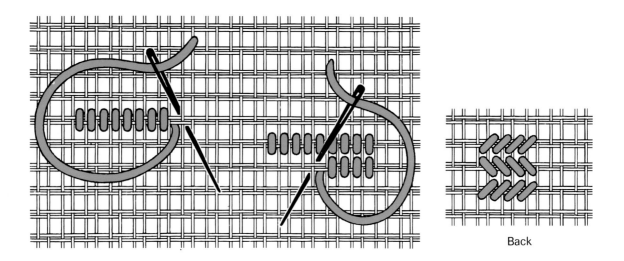

Back

Summary

a) From left to right (going): stitch between each vertical thread of the canvas, separating them regularly. Your stitches are vertical; the needle is slightly slanted, the eye toward the left.

b) From right to left (return): the stitches must be placed vertically, exactly below the stitches of the preceding row. The needle is slightly slanted, the eye toward the right.

This is a handsome, firm stitch, and it does not distort the canvas, as long as you work meticulously going and returning. It permits the adaptation-imitation of Aubusson or Gobelins designs (see the photograph and commentary on p.126) when one cannot order the reproduction from the Gobelins Manufactury — which is enormously expensive.

46

Straight Gobelin stitch *perlé* ("pearled" or backstitched)

When you use the regular Gobelin stitch for a backgound, on mono canvas over 2 meshes, the stitch may not perfectly cover the canvas; vertical threads may show between the rows of the Gobelin. These may be covered with a very fine line of backstitches to make an unusual and very effective "fancy" stitch. See also page 54.

Other stitches

One can mention the slanting Gobelin stitch and the encroaching slanting Gobelin, but we do not find them useful.

Finally, avoid absolutely what is called in French *le demi-point inversé*—which one stitches from right to left, horizontally, turning the canvas upside down to start each new row—and which Americans know as the Continental stitch*. This stitch uses a great deal of yarn, is very thick on the back of the canvas (which is illogical), and also badly distorts the canvas. Use the basketweave instead.

* However, it is worth noting the following: When you are doing detailed designs, the basketweave sometimes becomes impractical; to fill in tricky little areas, the half-cross stitch is recommended, but it may be used *only* on penelope canvas. On mono canvas, when it becomes impossible to stitch as regularly as the basketweave requires (or when outlining is required), then these small areas do have to be filled in with the Continental stitch, as the half-cross will slip under the intersections of canvas threads and will not cover them consistently. *(Ed.)*

Appropriate stitches for particular periods

Louis XIII	Repeat patterns Cross stitch Gros point (basketweave on a coarse canvas) Hungarian embroidery stitch (over 2 threads of the canvas)
Louis XIV	Gros point and petit point combined (basketweave) Counted stitches and repeat patterns
Louis XV Louis XVI	Petit point Basketweave, with or without petit point
Directoire Empire	Counted stitches and repeat patterns Straight Gobelin stitch Basketweave
Napoleon III	Combinations of stitches; repeat patterns Basketweave Straight Gobelin stitch

Practical advice

Errors to avoid in working

Before beginning to work, carefully list the colors of your yarn grouped by subject—especially if you are planning to depart from the color scheme suggested for the design you have selected.
As you work:

• Record the amount of yarn you used for one motif that is repeated; that will be a good indication of the total amount of yarn you will need.

• On cards keep a record of everything you do in the entire course of the work; this will keep you from making the same mistakes twice.

• Also be sure to make note of the little tricks that you yourself devise.

• Do not use too long a length of yarn on your needle; the yarn is liable to form knots and get frizzy, and it also gets damaged slightly in each passage through the canvas. If you are using a single thread of yarn, the ends may wear thin and even break in the course of repeated passages. If you are using the yarn in its full 3-thread strength, it may become matted. It always tends to coil up a little at each trip and after a certain number of stitches, you will have to rotate the needle between your thumb and index finger to let the yarn unwind. This is an extra operation, but it will restore the alignment of the yarn.

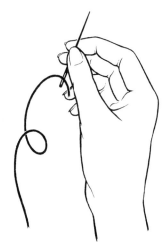

• Be careful not to insert your needle through the yarn of stitches in the preceding row; the needle should slip into the same hole, but *next* to the strand that is already there. An improperly placed stitch will not only spoil the appearance of the needlepoint but also will very much complicate any touching up at the end (there is often a great temptation to unravel and rework ugly stitches).

• The ideal of a good needleworker must be a work as neat and presentable on the back as on the front. Consequently, you must avoid sudden jumps—skipping on the wrong side from one motif to another with the excuse that they are the same color and close enough. The strands that have been thus stretched will pull back to their original length, pucker, and make proper blocking difficult and sometimes impossible. If you really are reluctant to stop (that is, to cut and begin again), slip the needle under stitches already worked, on the wrong side. Do not **pull.**
If you have been unable to resist making one of these jumps very loosely under a bare canvas, be sure to catch the yarn afterward, when you stitch the intervening space.

- From time to time, check on the evenness of your work by examining the back of the canvas. You will also find that the design the stitches form there will guide you if you are uncertain how to resume after you have stopped (see the explanations of the different stitches).

- If you are working without a frame, keep the canvas from distorting by stitching the central motif first (roll it as we have explained on p. 38 right side out).
Do not pull your stitches tightly; this will also **distort** the work—perhaps irretrievably.

- When you are left with a strand in your needle long enough to be used again, simply pull it through the edge of your canvas, and you will easily find it again.

- When you make a pattern of a chair, mark the location of the wooden upright so that you do not plan any ornament there. In working, however, you must stitch these areas just as completely as the visible parts; the upholsterer definitely prefers to have this extra allowance for safety. Actually, the canvas does the work; in stitching it, you draw it tighter; in placing it on the chair, the upholsterer stretches it—but not in exactly the same way. That is why we advise you to allow an extra margin for unforeseen eventualities.

- Never neglect the vertical edges of a chair in planning ornamentation. Give particular thought to the front of the chair; that is what first strikes the eye. Do not leave it plain unless you have a contrasting counterbackground. The design of the armrests must be in the proper position when you face the chair: stems of flowers toward the front, etc. And keep in mind how all the parts—back, seat, and arms—will appear to the spectator.

- A little "trick": when you do Gobelin stitch on a canvas that is a little large for the yarn (which is a very pleasant combination to work with), it is difficult to get a really dark background because the vertical threads of the canvas—which are either white or light tan—show through. To counteract this, mark them horizontally beforehand with an *indelible* marking pen in the appropriate color. We have already mentioned that because dark dye compresses the yarn, it often does not cover the threads of the canvas completely. The marking trick can also be used to remedy this. (Besides, the marking has the extra advantage of guiding your work.)

- Never make knots.

- Do not cut the end of your yarn too short (or stop too near the end); you should work the end of the thread under at least 6 or 7 stitches on the back. In blocking or putting the needlepoint on a chair, you risk trouble if you have not taken this precaution.

- On the other hand, do not leave long tails of yarn on the wrong side, thinking that they will give the work substance.

- As much as possible, avoid creating uneven thicknesses under your work when changing yarns, especially for the motifs.

- When you draw the pattern on the canvas, be extremely cautious if you are using a felt-tipped marking pen. It is essential to have one that is indelible; the ordinary marking pen will run at the first touch of water and come off on the yarn. If you use India ink, you will need a brush that is slightly stiff so that it will stand up in contact with the canvas—but be careful not to get any blots.

- Above all, never economize on the canvas. Besides the extra margins recommended for the pattern of the upholstery, allow plenty of additional canvas around the outside of the pattern—for whatever need may arise.

- If you are ironing your needlepoint with a pressing cloth, do not let the iron rest on your work; it will crush it instead of blocking it. If your needlepoint is to cover an entire chair, you should leave the blocking to the upholsterer.
For a cushion or bell pull, follow the instructions on page 53.

- If you use a frame, do not forget to unscrew it a half turn when you stop working so that the canvas is not stretched unnecessarily.

Order of work

Begin by stitching the motifs and details; work the background later. There is a good reason for this advice: it is hard to judge their effect before you actually stitch them. Moreover, if the background has been worked first and has encroached on the motif, it is extremely complicated to push it back to its proper limits. While you are still working the motif, it is infinitely easier to rip out a few ugly stitches or to correct a curve if there are no background stitches in your way.

However, as soon as you have stitched a sizable area of detail, you can begin to cover the backround simultaneously; that is, you can use a second needle threaded with the background color. Begin, naturally, in the upper right-hand corner. You may find it a relaxing change to work on the more automatic area of solid color after you have been involved for some time in the details of the design.

When you are doing the basketweave stitch, it is logical to begin with the first motif at the upper right and work downward and outward.

With the half-cross stitch, you can begin with the central motif and work starwise over the canvas, since you can turn the work upside down at will.

In Gobelin stitch, you work downward, starting at the top of the motif or motifs.

When you have covered a certain area of Gobelin, you can attack the background simultaneously, beginning at the upper left, with the first horizontal "going" row.

Note: It is better to work regularly, even only for fifteen minutes every day, than to drive yourself to stitch for three solid hours on Sunday. Every detail, every movement that has been useful, will then stay clear in your mind.

Finishing—touching up

You have now covered the entire canvas.

Check that all the threads have been safely caught in before you cut off the ends that are still dangling on the back of your work.

Hold the work up in front of the light, like a transparency. Undoubtedly you will discover skipped stitches that let light come through. Mark the spot on the outside; you will easily find it with the end of your nail. To fill in these gaps, split a strand of the yarn, and use only 1 thread. Catch the beginning of the thread under several stitches on the back. Fix the missing (or imperfect) stitches, going over each stitch twice or more to get the proper thickness. Catch the end of the thread in the usual way and cut it flush with the canvas. Touching up with split yarn avoids lumps made by beginning and ending the thread.

If you have made the pattern for your chair too small, and you have to add on a strip or a band of extra stitches, be careful about the point where it will be joined. If it is only for the inner fold, it is not serious; that will be covered by the nails or the edging and will not be under strain. But if the band to be added is visible, you must be certain that the pattern is maintained on the wrong side. To avoid a weak point at the joining, whenever you work up to the edge of the existing needlepoint, turn it to the wrong side, slide the needle under the last stitch of the original work, and hook your new stitch onto it.

For basketweave stitch, you must re-create the effect of weaving on the back. This is a small but important refinement. Proceed in the same way for spaces to be filled in.

When you have to undo a considerable area that has been worked, begin by cutting a stitch in the middle of each row to be ripped. Then pull the yarn with the end of the needle from the front and from the back (which is easier). Rip out enough so that you can catch in the yarn at the end of each row by slipping it under the adjacent stitches. Fill in the bare spots with split yarn if only a few stitches are involved, keep the to full number of threads of the strand you have been using if a larger area is involved, but watch out for extra thickness when you start and end.

How to join squares and bands

First we assume that you have not stitched up to the very edge but have left 1 1/2 inches unworked to give you room for joining.

We also assume that you have measured exactly, since the squares or bands to be joined must be the same size in order for the meshes of the two pieces of canvas to line up precisely. Now you must block or steam each of the pieces to be joined. If you steam the needlepoint, do it lightly, using a pressing cloth and not letting the iron rest on it. This step evens out the stitches and shrinks the canvas a little, which does no harm.

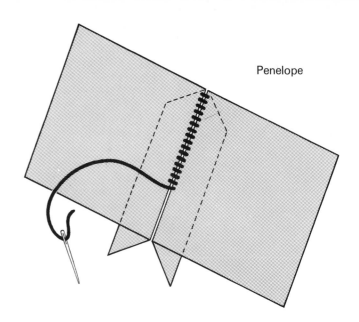

Penelope

I. For penelope:

Fold the edge of each of the pieces to be joined carefully between one pair of the close threads of the canvas. Crease the fold with your nail.

Joining: The meshes of the canvas must be matched up on the right side of the needlepoint as we said above. Sew edge to edge (see the diagram).

II. For mono canvas:

Make a rough fold and crease it with your fingernail along one thread of the canvas; this will give you a guide for joining the two pieces.

Joining: Work edge to edge in backstitch, carefully matching meshes (see the diagram). Open the seam and check whether the meshes are matched up.

In both cases you can conceal the joining with binding stitches of the proper depth.

After you have finished the joining, catch the stitches securely into each other, on the wrong side, without interfering with the pattern. Steam the work again to even it out.

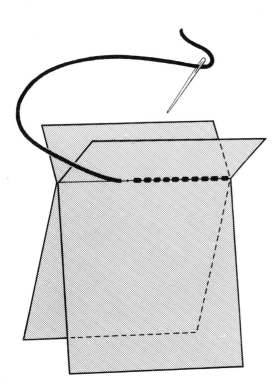

Mono canvas

52

How to block finished needlepoint

The canvas always gets more or less out of shape when you work without a frame, and it also "shrinks" somewhat, depending on the stitch you use. With the Gobelin stitch, for instance, the canvas does not become biased, but it is noticeably shortened.

You do not need an upholsterer to put your work back into shape unless it is a large piece of upholstery. What you will need is an absolutely clean wooden board, a piece of fine white cloth (it does not have to be new), pure water (rainwater or distilled water), a stapler and stainless-steel staples, or rustproof tacks. If you have a steam iron, that is perfect.

Lay the needlepoint wrong side up on the white fabric. Tack or staple the top of the canvas very evenly to the board (if your board is really square, you can use the top and a side of it as your guide). Lightly dampen the back of the needlepoint or—better—steam it without resting the iron on it.

The canvas will become soft and you will be able to pull gradually at it until it is the right shape.

Mark where the left corner should go and fasten it there on the board. Then, one after another, fasten sides 2, 3, and 4, following the diagram. Put it to dry flat, away from extreme heat, for two or three days. The little bumps and other imperfections will have vanished as if by magic.

Note: If you use tacks, not do push them all the way in, so that it will be easier to take them out. If you use staples, be careful not to leave sharp ends in the board when you remove them.

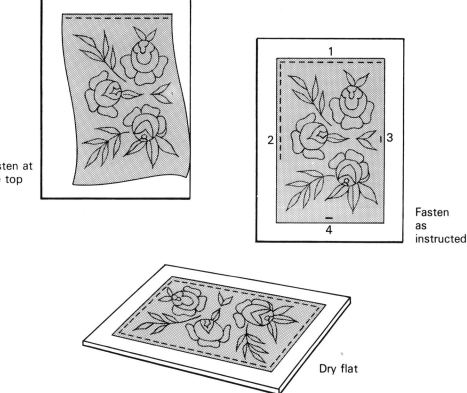

Fasten at the top

Fasten as instructed

Dry flat

Chart of canvases, Persian yarn, and stitches

The best needlepoint canvases sold in the United States are imported from Europe. However, our needlepoint shops do not use the European identifications for mesh sizes of canvas, but rather identify them by the number of canvas meshes (spaces between threads) or threads (hence stitches) that the canvas holds per inch. This chart lists only the canvases that are most readily available in this country and was tested for how, for each canvas, one should split or add to strands of Paternayan Persian yarn. *(Ed.)*

Penelope canvas / Persian yarn

no. 10/20
- Basketweave, **1 strand**
- Petit point, basketweave (20 stitches to the inch), **1 thread**
- Half-cross stitch, **1 strand**
- Straight Gobelin over 2 canvas threads, **1 strand plus 1 thread**
- Straight Gobelin *perlé,* over 2 canvas threads, **1 strand;** backstitch between the rows with **1 thread**
- Straight Gobelin, worked parallel to the selvage, "splitting" the canvas, **1 strand**

no. 7/14
- Basketweave, **2 strands**
- Petit point, basketweave (14 stitches to the inch), **2 threads**
- Cross-stitch, **1 strand**
  (Since this is a rug canvas, other stitches are not likely to be suitable.)

Mono canvas / Persian yarn

no. 18 Petit point, basketweave, **1 thread**

no. 14
- Basketweave, **2 threads**
- Straight Gobelin over 2 canvas threads, **1 strand**
- Counted stitches (pp. 55-59), **1 strand;** no. 14 canvas is the most convenient for counted stitches with Persian yarn

no. 12
- Basketweave, **2 threads,** but test the canvas; some no. 12 mono is nearer 11 than 12 mesh to the inch and may require **1 strand,** especially for background areas
- Straight Gobelin over 2 meshes, **1 strand**
- Straight Gobelin *perlé,* over 2 canvas threads, **1 strand;** backstitch between the rows with **1 thread**
- Counted stitches (pp. 55-59), **1 strand or 1 strand plus 1 thread,** depending on the particular stitch and the "looseness" of the canvas

no. 10
- Basketweave, **1 strand,** but test the canvas; some no. 10 mono is nearer 9 than 10 mesh to the inch and may require **1 strand plus 1 thread,** especially for background areas
- Straight Gobelin over 2 canvas threads, **1 strand plus 1 thread**
- Straight Gobelin *perlé,* over 2 canvas threads, **1 strand;** backstitch between the rows with **2 threads**
- Counted stitches (pp. 55-59), **1 strand plus 1 thread** or **plus 2 threads,** depending on the particular stitch and the "looseness" of the canvas

Note: The cross stitch and the half-cross stitch cannot be done on mono canvas. *(Ed.)*

Mono canvases nos. 14, 12, and 10, and penelope canvas no. 10/20 are all suitable for upholstery and for pillows and many other projects. No. 18 is very fine and is to be used for small, detailed projects; it may be used for pillows if you wish. The no. 7/14 penelope rug canvas may also be used for quick projects including pillows. Mono no. 10 and penelope no. 10/20 are used for rugs by most needlepointers unless a "quick" rug is wanted.

COUNTED STITCHES, REPEAT PATTERNS, AND PERIOD BANDS

After you have worked all the central motifs of your needlepoint, you may decide that you would like to make the background lighter or darker than you had originally planned—but without changing your color scheme since you are so far along with your work. You can do this merely by using a decorative "fancy" stitch, because its highlights and shadows will create a different effect from that produced by a flat filler stitch such as basketweave.

We suggest that you experiment with various background effects that are possible with some traditional counted stitches. Their poetic names testify to their origins. Try them out on a separate piece of canvas, look at your samples in a good light (never in sunlight), holding them vertically, as they would appear on the back of the chair, and flat, as on the seat. Compare the different effects before choosing. (It is not a heresy to switch to a different stitch for the background; there are many examples of this kind of combination on chairs whose covers date from the eighteenth century.)

There are several stitches that are flat enough to suit all designs: Parisian, Renaissance, diagonal Florentine, straight encroaching Gobelin. Or try the Bargello *point mosaïque,* but in one color; it will sparkle alongside a design of large flowers.

Give particular consideration to the Florentine or flame stitch; we give only one simple example, but all the variants are suitable for period chairs. The length of the stitches in this pattern can be increased, the colors changed and multiplied. You can twist it into waves and it becomes the *point de Chine* ("Chinese stitch"). Variants are often called Bargello. In bygone times, elaborate variations of this stitch covered whole walls. See also how the diagonal Florentine stitch is transformed when it is worked in two colors (no. 3 and 15 on pp. 56-59). We also show you four repeat patterns that are more difficult to execute than the fancy stitches because they are more elaborate. However, they are extremely decorative. Study them carefully. After a little practice, they no longer seem hard. You may find it helpful to mark guidepoints on your canvas (in the past this was done with silk stitches that were taken out in the course of the work). If you work these repeat patterns on a coarse canvas, with the yarn doubled or with thick yarn (for example, a no. 7 canvas with 2 strands of Persian wool), you will get a stunning effect and the work will go very quickly. If you work repeat patterns in cross stitch, you will achieve beautiful, symmetrical results; try this with the Louis XIII "carnation" or "vine leaves" motifs. In addition, all of these patterns lend themselves to use in bands *(galons)* of various widths. You need only provide a narrow border on each side of the repeat pattern you use.

Such needlepoint bands contribute an individual touch to furniture. They may be used on all kinds of chairs, from Louis XIII to contemporary. They can decorate the edges of stools and the flat seat pads known as *galettes.* They make bell pulls or tiebacks for curtains; they trim hangings or shades. They can cover mantelpieces and piano keys, and decorate almost any piece of furniture you have.

Note: All these counted stitches may be done on either mono or penelope canvas. However, some are shown on mono, others on penelope because the stitch is rendered somewhat better on the one or the other. *(Ed.)*

Background stitches

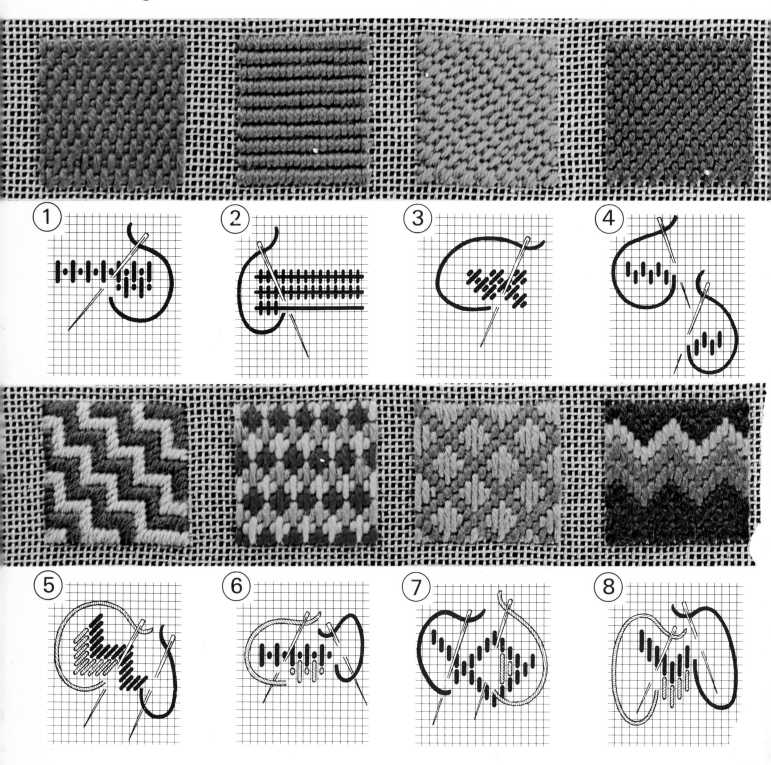

① Parisian embroidery stitch *(point de Paris)*

1st row: Make 1 long upright (vertical) stitch over 3 threads of the canvas, followed by 1 short upright stitch over 1 thread of the canvas; 1 long stitch, etc.
2nd row: Alternate 1 short upright stitch below 1 long; 1 long below 1 short, etc.

② Renaissance stitch *(point Renaissance)*

This is worked horizontally over 2 threads of the canvas.
1st row: Lay a tramé thread from right to left. Make upright stitches from left to right over 2 threads of the canvas and over the tramé thread (which pads the stitch).
2nd row: The same.

③ Diagonal Florentine or diagonal mosaic stitch *(point de Florence* or *point de velours)*

1st row: Alternate the long stitch, covering 2 intersections of threads of the canvas, with the short stitch, which covers 1 intersection.
2nd row: Alternate the short and long stitches, reversing the order.

④ Straight encroaching Gobelin or brick stitch *(point Gobelin empiétant)*

Although this gives a zigzag effect, it is worked in upright stitches, over 2 horizontal threads of the canvas, with alternating points of entry. (It is, therefore, also known as the alternating stitch.) You proceed in both directions, from left to right and back again.

⑤ Byzantine stitch *(point Jacquart)* in two tones

Study the diagram carefully. The stitch is diagonal, laid in sequence to form a zigzag. Each stitch diagonally covers 2 horizontal threads of the canvas. The pattern is formed by vertical rows of 5 stitches alternating with horizontal rows of 5 stitches.

⑥ Hungarian embroidery stitch *(point Hongrois* or *fleur de lys)* in three tones

1st row: (from left to right) using dark tone: 1 long upright stitch over 3 threads of the canvas, 1 short upright stitch over 1 thread of the canvas, etc.
2nd row: (from right to left) using medium tone: repeat, alternating the lengths of stitches in reverse order (short, long, short, etc.).
3rd row: (from left to right) using pale tone: repeat, alternating the lengths of stitches and reversing the order again (long, short, long, etc.).

⑦ Bargello stitch in a "diamond" variant *(point mosaïque)* in two colors

This is a variant of the Hungariant embroidery stitch, and itself has many variations.
1st color: Begin at the upper left and work the outline of the diamonds: make 5 upright stitches, working downward (each over 2 threads of the canvas); then, working upward toward the right, make 4 more upright stitches of the same length (over 2 threads of the canvas). Continue the pattern of 4 stitches up and 4 down to the end of the row. Then, working from right to left, complete the bottom half of the outline of the diamonds.
2nd color: Fill in the 5 vertical spaces inside the diamonds, using upright stitches over 2 to 6 threads of the canvas, to form the central lozenge.

⑧ Florentine or flame stitch *(point de Hongrie)* shown in dark green, gold, and rust

The pattern consists of rows of the three colors, worked to the depths you want. (A variation of this pattern is used for design 1, pp. 72 ff.)
1st row (gold): Work in upright stitches over 2 threads of the canvas; every fifth stitch, shift direction: down, up, down, etc.
2nd and 3rd rows (rust): Work as for 1st row, repeating so that you have 2 rows of this color.
4th, 5th rows, etc. (dark green): Work as for 1st row, repeating so that you have the desired number of rows of this color.

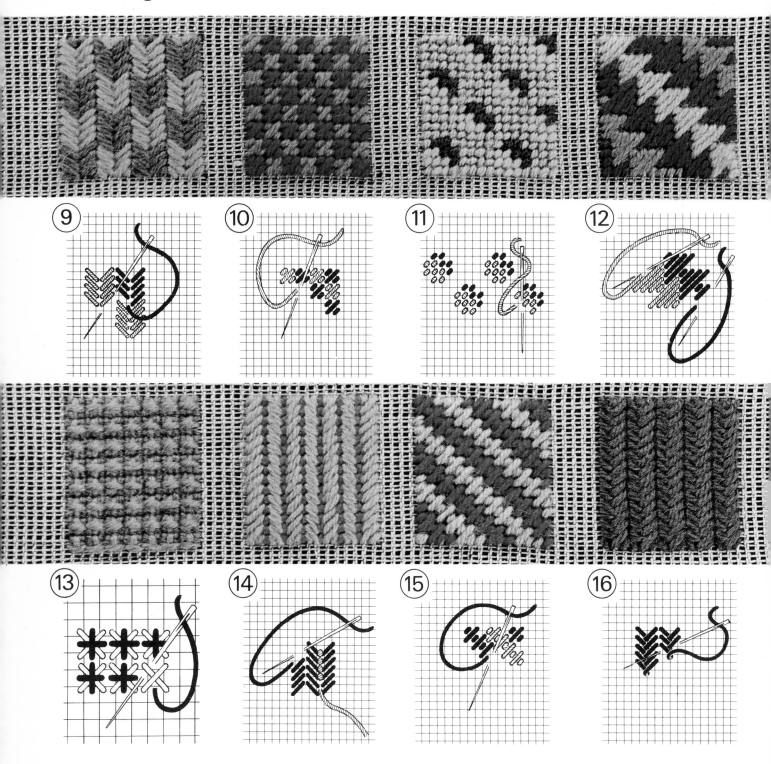

⑨ Chevron stitch *(point de chevrons)* shown in gold and green

This is worked from right to left; you can make several chevrons of the same color in a row or step them off, proceeding at an angle. Study the diagram carefully. We began with the gold chevron at the right, worked an entire pattern (4 stitches down and 4 up), and then we proceeded with the same color up to the left. We worked the green chevrons in the same sequence.

⑩ Mosaic stitch *(point mosaïque d'Orient)* in two colors

1st color (from upper right): Make one square with 1 short diagonal stitch (over 1 intersection of threads of the canvas), 1 long diagonal (over 2 intersections), 1 short diagonal stitch, etc.
2nd color: Work 3 squares—directly to the left of and directly below the first.
1st color (third set of squares): Work 3 squares fitted in next to the squares of the 2nd color, starting directly to the left and working downward, etc.

⑪ Shadowed polka dot *(le pois et son ombre)* shown in gold, dark brown, and pale jade green

In this repeat pattern, the gold polka dot is made with 7 basketweave stitches: 2 on the first row, 3 on the next, and 2 on the third. The shadow is made with 2 and 3 stitches. Study the pattern counting (vertically) 6 stitches between the starting points of the polka dots, etc.

⑫ Milanese stitch *(point de Milan)* shown in three colors

This is worked diagonally from left to right going down and then up from right to left.
1st color: Make triangles consisting of 4 stitches of increasing length (over 1, 2, 3, and 4 intersections), working downward.
2nd color: Make triangles of 4 stitches of increasing length, but proceeding in the reverse direction—working upward.
3rd color: Working downward again, make triangles again with 4 stitches of increasing length, placed next to the triangles of the 2nd color, etc. *

⑬ Smyrna cross or single Leviathan stitch *(point de diable* or *Croix de Smyrne)* in two colors

This stitch is done in two steps:
(a) With the darker color, make a row of diagonal cross stitches over 3 threads of the canvas; the threads will cross at the center over an empty square.
(b) With the lighter color, make perpendicular crosses over the diagonal crosses. Be careful that the crosses on top are all stitched in the same direction (horizontal *over* vertical).

⑭ Stem stitch with running backstitch *(point de tige)* in two colors

(a) Work from right to left of the canvas, going up on the right side of the "stem," slanting the stitches over 2 intersections of the threads of the canvas. Work back down the left side of the stem, slanting the stitches in the opposite direction.
(b) When the surface has been covered, with the second color re-embroider with short vertical backstitches at each mesh where the long slanting stitches meet.

⑮ Diagonal Florentine or diagonal mosaic stitch *(point de Florence)* in two colors

This is worked on a slant, with short and long stitches alternating regularly (over 1 and 2 intersections of threads of the canvas). In the 2nd row, the 2nd color is used, and the order of long and short stitches is reversed, so that a short stitch is placed next to a long stitch of the preceding row, etc.

⑯ Fern stitch *(point de fougère)*

This pattern is formed by successive rows worked from top to bottom. Starting with the left half of the stitch, the needle first goes diagonally downward from the left over the intersection 2 threads of the canvas away. It hooks *under* the vertical, and then slants diagonally upward to form the right side of the stitch. The stitches are all the same length, extending over 2 intersections of the canvas.

Period repeat-pattern designs

Louis XIII carnation in cross stitch

Penelope canvas
Background: Pale pink beige: no. 271
Outline: Dark brown: no. 115

From top to bottom
1st design (complete):
Pale ocher: no. 457; Light rust: no. 433; Dark gray green: no. 516; Medium russet: no. 274
2nd design (complete):
Pale blue green (2 tones): no. 395 and 350; Bright dark blue: no. 312; Peach beige: no. 257
3rd design (incomplete):
Peach beige: no. 257; Medium russet: no. 274; Dark gray green: no. 516; Light ocher: no. 433
Stitch the outline first, counting the stitches carefully.

Louis XIII vine leaves in cross stitch

Penelope canvas
Background: Bright maroon: no. 231
Leaves: Light olive green: no. 533
Begin by stitching the leaves; then fill in the background.

You can devise other combinations; for example, gold on a green background, pink on a gray background, two pinks in a monochrome scheme, etc.

Louis XVI latticework with roses in bloom in basketweave

Mono canvas
Mark some guidepoints on the canvas: for example, the center of the roses and the intersection of the lattices.

Background: Pale beige: no. 153
Latticework and stems: Dark olive green: no. 540
Roses: Rust (2 tones): no. 274 and 286; Old rose: no. 245
Leaves: Light green brown: no. 531

Louis XVI latticework with miniature roses in basketweave

Mono canvas
Mark some guidepoints on the canvas, as above: the center of the roses and the intersection of the lattices.

Background: Pale beige: no. 153
Latticework: Olive green: no. 450
Roses: Brick red (2 tones): no. 225 and 269
Stems: Dark gray green: no. 516
Leaves: Apple green: no. 553

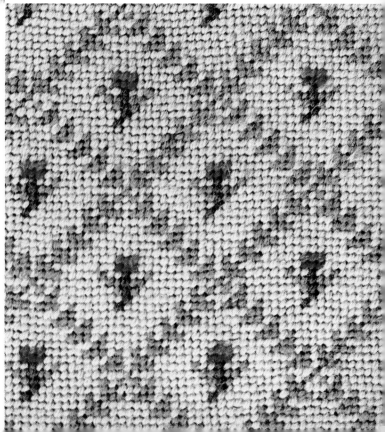

Period bands *(galons)*

A prime attraction of needlepoint bands is that they can be completed very much more quickly than a whole chair or even a single cushion. And you will find that they are remarkably effective in brightening up your furniture and coordinating your decorative scheme. Some of the ways in which you can use bands are illustrated here, and we show you four different period designs that you can adapt to your own needs. You can change the colors, of course, but be sure to stay within the spirit of the period.

When you prepare the canvas at the start, allow a border of at least $1\frac{1}{2}$ inches all around the area of the design. To prevent the edges from raveling, hem them or bind with masking tape or cotton binding.

In finishing the needlepoint band, the method you choose will vary according to the purpose for which the band is to be used.

For a bell pull or piano keyboard cover, *either:*

(a) fold the edge back onto the wrong side along the last 2 or 3 rows of completed stitches. Baste the canvas in place. Set the hem by steaming it lightly, using a press cloth. Then fasten it with a whipstitch and sewing thread, without letting your stitches show on the right side. Make a silk or felt lining, folding the raw edge in underneath, to measure about $\frac{1}{4}$ inch less all around than the needlepoint piece. Blindstitch the lining to the back of the needlepoint;

or (b) fold the edge of the canvas, leaving a row of meshes that has not been worked along the stitched edge. Crease this fold with your fingernail, and stitch the hem to the back by overcasting. Go over the edge of the unworked canvas with a binding stitch. Make a lining, following the instructions for method (a) above.

To place the band on an upholstered chair and hide the edge with braid, fold the band along the stitched edge, and fasten the hem back by overcasting. Glue or stitch the braid so that it overlaps the point where the band meets the upholstery fabric. If the band must make perfectly square corners, do not try to fold the straight piece into right angles. Instead, cut four separate piece so that they can be joined in precise miters (see the instructions under "How to join squares and bands," p.52).

A and D: Napoleon III
B and C: Empire

A

B

C

D

EXECUTION
Choosing the design

Consider the period.

Consider the **wood** the furniture is made of. If it is very elaborately carved and gilded, choose a design with plain lines or an airy, open pattern (see the "Armchair à la reine," pp.18 and 78).

If the wood is carved, try to find a design in which one or two details (or the design as a whole) will seem to **match**— or at least be in harmony. See the photograph of the Louis XV cabriole with the bouquet on p.89: the roses and the little flowers have been especially designed to complement the sculptured motifs of the wood— round roses, round florets, and florets with pointed petals, etc.

Consider the **stitches** (see the table of the relationship of periods and stitches, p 47).

If you do not have a great deal of experience—or a great deal of courage—choose a monochromatic *camaïeu* design and use a simple stitch. If you execute it with care, you will find the effect very satisfying.

Think about designs with **repeat patterns.** They enable you to achieve a remarkable range of effects, and they lend themselves to innumerable uses.

If you like the **design** of one of our chairs but not the colors, do not hesitate to substitute a color scheme that you prefer.

You may want to use only a **detail** from a design. You can easily make the detail very large and immediately you have a design for a pillow. You can work it with fine yarn (with large plain areas) or, on the contrary, with thick yarn, and canvas to match of course.

Colors

Each period requires its own gamut of colors. However, it is possible to take some liberties. In needlework, as in painting, one seldom uses black black and a white that is truly white. (We are not speaking here of very modern needlework in which everything is permitted and the colors are often very harsh.)
In the romantic epoch, nevertheless, bouquets or wreaths of flowers on a black background were very popular. For these designs, somber dull shades such as chocolate, *nègre,* midnight blue, or very dark garnet will have an appropriately subdued effect. White is replaced by faintly creamy ecru, but all the off-white shades can be introduced: bluish, greenish, pinkish, straw-like, etc.

For period chairs, it is important to consider the tone of the wood—especially if it is lacquered. The background of the needlepoint may be chosen from the same family of colors as the wood, but you can also create a contrast of one tone setting off the other : for a cool tone in the lacquer, a warm background, and vice versa .What is essential is to find a color scheme that will neither be too dreary nor too garish.

Remember that lights and shadows fall differently on the high and low points of your stitches. The overall appearance of the design is also affected by the size of the stitches :the smaller the stitches, the more intense the colors appear.

Note: After the yarn has been worked, it always looks a little darker than it does in the skein.

How to make a pattern for your chair.

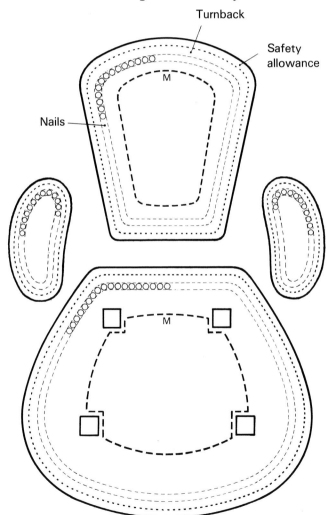

Turnback

Safety allowance

Nails

M

M

If the chair to be recovered has lost some of its stuffing and springiness, remember to take that into consideration when measuring:
(1) for the **back,** it is necessary to make the canvas a little larger than the actual measurements;
(2) for the **bottom,** it will be helpful to slide a stool under the seat, to raise the webbing a little and restore it to an approximation of its true size.Do not outline the pattern until after you have done this. To the back, pin a piece of cloth of any kind (an old sheet will do). Using an indelible marking pen, trace the outline of the upholstery up to the nails.With a pencil, outline the central area in which you will work the chief motif. (This *motif* surface is designated *M* in the illustration.) Small designs can extend outside this boundary all around, and you will, of course, stitch the canvas at least 2 inches beyond the turnback as a safety allowance.

For the *armrests,* you need to take only one impression. The pattern of the second armrest will be a mirror image of the first.

If your chair has arms, you must take an extra step in measuring the seat. Slit the cloth for the pattern a few inches in from the four corners, up to the wood of the armposts and of the back. Cut it so that it will lie completely flat. Carefully pin the central area which you will mark with a pencil (just as you did for the back). This will ensure that the main motif will be placed inside the four wooden posts and that its symmetry will not be broken by them. With a felt-tipped pen, trace the overall outline up to the nails. Note carefully how the corners are treated: are they completely covered with the upholstery pattern or does the wood show through? For a chair without arms, fold the "pattern" in at the corners so that you can mark their position and avoid planning any ornament there.

For stools of various shapes, use the same method: mark out the horizontal surface for the main motif, the width of the borders to be worked, the overlap for the corners.

Materials needed

A drawing board (a piece of plywood will serve) and some white paper to cover it.

For the sketch, a few sheets of large white paper sturdy enough to be erased without tearing.

Good quality tracing paper marked *in centimeters* (this is *essential;* see p. 67);

A long ruler and a T square to draw the grids.

A soft pencil, an eraser, a blue pencil, an indelible black marking pen or India ink and a penpoint that is not too flexible. (Check *very* carefully whether the marking pen is really indelible. Do not take the manufacturer's word for it. Test it on a piece of canvas and let it dry thoroughly. Then rub it with a wet cloth. If it blurs at all, do not use it; you risk muddying your colors if the ink runs in the blocking.)

One or two cushions on which to lean the drawing board.

Transferring the pattern onto paper

You have now cut a kind of "pattern" of each of the pieces of upholstery on the chair that you are going to recover. Fasten the paper for the sketch to the drawing board and tack the center of the pattern for the seat to the center of the paper. Tack the pattern smoothly all around. (You will later follow this same procedure for the back and armrests.) Draw the outline and enlarge it with 4 lines to indicate:

1) the width of the nails

2) the turnback

3) the safety allowance (1 $\frac{1}{2}$- 2 inches), which will be stitched in needlepoint

4) a 2-inch allowance of blank canvas at the outer edge, where it will be bound or hemmed to prevent raveling.

You must indicate on the sketch the positions of the wooden portions of the chair in order to center the design between them and not plan any ornament there. Lightly mark the *M* area inside these wooden portions in which you will place the main design.

Note: Old chairs have often gotten a little out of shape in the course of time. Do not try to duplicate all these variations. Merely straighten out the pattern and draw the outlines symmetrically. When the upholsterer puts the needlepoint on the chair, he will adjust it to fit the frame.

DRAWING THE DESIGN YOU HAVE CHOSEN

...on paper

On sketch paper you now have marked off both areas of the design proper. With the T square, draw a vertical and a horizontal line through the center points of back and seat with the blue pencil (they must be exactly perpendicular to each other and straight on the paper). Label them «center line» at all four edges of the paper. Measure the design proper of the seat in the *book* at its *maximum width;* and measure the design area at the same point on the *paper pattern.* Let us say the widest point of the design in the book measures 22 centimeters and the same point on the pattern measures 66 centimeters. Divide the book dimension *into* the pattern dimension (66 centimeters divided by 22 equals 3). That 3 means that the squares on the grid you will draw on the paper pattern must be *three times* the size of the squares on the book page. The squares on the book page measure 1 centimeter, therefore the squares you will draw on the paper will measure 3 centimeters.

The same enlargement should fit for the back when you come to draw the grid for that; however, to be sure, do this: Measure the design proper of the back in the *book* at its *maximum height.* Let us say it is 15 centimeters; multiply 15 by 3, which equals 45 centimeters. On a chair of good proportions and appropriate to the design you have selected for it, the 45 centimeters for the height of the design should be just about what you already have on its paper pattern.

However, if the vertical dimension for the back is definitely too large, reverse the whole procedure. Take the dimension for the maximum height you actually have on the pattern, and divide *that* by the 15 centimeters, or whatever the corresponding measure is in the *book.* You will now get a new, smaller figure for the dimension of the squares of both grids you will draw—for you will now also draw the grid for the seat with these smaller squares, thus reducing the design on the seat from what you had first thought it would be. But this is correct; the relationships between parts of the design must remain the same on seat and back as the designer planned them. This can only be done with identical grids for both.

Now to explain why you *must* have a long ruler marked in centimeters and millimeters; (these are sold in American art-supply and engineering drafting-supply stores). When you measure a dimension in the book and divide it into the corresponding dimension on the chair pattern, you will frequently get a result with a decimal (22 into 66 equals 3 was a hypothetical example likely to be too good to be true). Figuring what to do

Model (scale: $^1/1.8$ cm.)

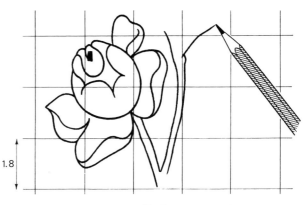

Design

67

with this decimal in fractions of *inches* is an arithmetical nightmare. With centimeters—the decimal part of which is the millimeter—the exact counterpart of your arithmetic is plain to see right on the ruler. Therefore, the American edition of this book keeps the 1-centimeter blue grid on the design pages specifically to make the process of squaring up easier, not harder.

Draw the grids on the paper patterns with the T square and blue pencil, using the center lines already drawn as the starting points. *(Ed.)*

Enlarging by squaring up

Study the diagram. For each small square on the grid, there must be a large square on the sketch paper. Note where the lines of the design intersect the small squares of the diagram, and use them as guidepoints in reproducing the design on your sketch paper (see the illustration).

First draw the main outlines in pencil, square by square. Then add the details with a fine line. Step back and judge it from a distance.

Redraw anything that seems to bother you. If the outside edges (the vertical borders of the seat) seem too bare, let a few little flowers or a graceful spray of foliage slip out onto them. Or add an arabesque. On the other hand, if the design seems too crowded or busy, eliminate or reduce part of it.

After these finishing touches, go over the main lines with black marking pen, do the details with a finer line, and erase the rough pencil outline. You now have the final drawing.

... on tracing paper

Put a piece of tracing paper over this final drawing. Mark the mid-points and the outer edge. Carefully trace the design with a black marking pen, using a finer line for the details in order to make certain that they are sharp. If the design is symmetrical, you can take a shortcut by tracing only the right half of the design. Then take off the tracing paper, and remove the sketch. Fold the tracing paper vertically, matching up the edges, with the drawn side face out. Place the folded tracing paper—with the unmarked side up—on the white paper fastened to the drawing board. You can now trace the other half of the design very easily. When you unfold the tracing paper, your drawing will be as sharp on the left as on the right.

Enlarging by photostat

A more expensive but unquestionably easier and far more accurate method of enlarging designs—as opposed to squaring up—is to have the enlargement done by photostat. You order *positive* stats, from which you can transfer directly onto canvas without making any grid or doing any prior drawing and tracing. (You need not worry about the blue grid lines in the book; they are not visible to the photostat camera and will not appear on the stat.)

First, you do the same arithmetic as for squaring up (p. 67), but you use *inches,* not centimeters, and you do the arithmetic only to check that both seat and back designs will fit on your particular chair.

Measure the seat design proper at its *widest point* in the *book*. To use hypothetical numbers again, say the widest point measures 8 inches. Now measure this same dimension for the design proper on the *paper pattern* you have made (pp. 65-66). Say the pattern dimension is 24 inches. Divide the book dimension *into* the pattern dimension (24 divided by 8 equals 3). The 3 means your seat design will be three times larger over all than it is in the book. (If the division gives you a figure with a decimal, no problem; just use the figure, carried to about two or three digits past the decimal point, for the next step. After that, you won't have to think about it again.)

Now test that the design proper of the back will fit. Measure the back design proper at its *maximum height* in the *book*. Multiply this by 3, or whatever the figure was that you got above. You should get a number that corresponds just about to the maximum height for the design proper on your paper pattern. If so, now go to the photostat shop and ask to have the design for the *seat* enlarged into a positive stat exactly the number of *inches* at its widest point that you have established you want. Then ask to have the design proper for the back enlarged *to the same scale*, or by the same percentage, which means the same thing to the photostater. The photostat camera will do this automatically.

If the design for the back proved *too large* when you did the testing arithmetic, don't do any more figuring. Just tell the photostat shop that you want the design proper for the *back* enlarged to the number of *inches* that *do* fit as drawn on your paper pattern at the point of *maximum height*. Then ask that the *seat* be enlarged to the same scale i.e., by the same percentage. Again, this will happen automatically. The seat design will come out a little smaller than you had originally figured, but this is as it should be (p. 67).

When you get your photostats, locate their center points and center lines and tape them with transparent tape onto the paper patterns, lining them up with the patterns' center lines. The photostats will be very clear and there is no need to trace them onto tracing paper as is necessary with hand-drawn designs.

The drawings in this book are impeccably made. The American editors strongly recommend that you use the photostat process to transfer them in accurate detail to your canvas.

You may find that some photostat shops refuse to make a print of a design because of the copyright notice in the front of the book, stating that photographic reproduction of material in the book is prohibited. This is a misunderstanding on the part of the shop. The provision is not meant to apply to individual use for a single, private purpose, such as your own needlepoint. It is designed to prevent multiple *distribution* of material from a copyrighted source which does not compensate the copyright holder for such distribution. *(Ed.)*

Preparing the canvas before the drawing is transferred

After the tracing is finished, measure off the area of the canvas you will need, being careful to allow for a 2-inch border all around on each piece.

Remember that the canvas is *not* the same in both directions. The selvages are on the right and left; the warp threads are vertical. (In penelope, the warp threads are closer together than the woof threads.) Pieces for upholstery must run vertically (except if you are doing the small Gobelin stitch on penelope canvas, for which you **deliberately** turn the canvas in the wrong direction). This ensures that the distortion (or biasing) of the canvas will be the same for all the pieces. This applies to both penelope and mono canvas.

Canvas also has a wrong and a right side, although the difference is often almost imperceptible. Usually, the right side is **inside** the rolled piece. However, it is better to check which side has small defects—little knots, thin threads. You can "lose" them more easily on the wrong side.

Begin by cutting off the selvages; they will constrict the canvas and distort its shape. (But be **sure** on mono canvas that you mark the direction of the vertical warp threads; it is virtually impossible to tell which is a warp or weft after the selvage is cut off, yet your canvas **will** be distorted if you work it in the wrong direction. *(Ed.)* Cut the canvas into rectangles for the different pieces of the chair. Fold about $1/4$ inch in toward the wrong side of the canvas, following along the same line of thread—this is important. Crease the fold between your fingernails. Stitch it on the machine, right side up, going over it twice with fairly large stitches. This will prevent the edge from raveling. You can also put a strip of masking tape around the edges of the canvas without folding it in. This method is certainly faster but less secure.

Transferring the drawing to the canvas

Now that you have traced the drawing onto the tracing paper precisely as you want it on the canvas, tack the tracing paper onto the white paper that covers the drawing board. Then at the top of the canvas, mark the mid-point with a small vertical line (using an indelible marking pen or India ink). Run your fingernail down the canvas, following the same thread, to the mid-point at the bottom. Do the same to mark the horizontal mid-points. Now place the canvas on the tracing paper in such a way that both mid-points—the axes—are lined up. You may find that you have to pull the canvas more on one side than on the other to make the guidepoints align. To see the drawing clearly through the canvas, slant the board. Turn your back slightly away from the window so that the light falls onto the canvas. Find the best angle for the work.

First draw the main outlines and major details. If the fine points are hard to see, leave them to be added later. *Note:* If the design is symmetrical, you can check it by running your fingertip along a horizontal thread; you should have exactly the same motifs at that point on each side. As you repeat this test a few times, you will not find absolutely identical placement of the design for each thread here and there—but it should be very similar.

After the drawing is on the canvas

If you are working on mono canvas, it is essential to study the color photograph of the design carefully; the photograph is your guide to color placement throughout the stitching process. On cards, note the details of the colors specified, subject by subject. If that does not seem helpful, practice by working one motif separately—especially if it is to be repeated several times—on a small piece of canvas. Choose a flower, a leaf, an arabesque. That will establish your personal style, and you will find this example handy for reference.

If you are working on penelope, you can tramé the motifs. This will make the final execution easier, and it will, in addition, pad the details and set them off. (See the explanation of "Half-cross stitch tramé" p. 43.)

If you tramé the entire design beforehand, you can have a preview of the overall effect—a sort of "color sketch" in wool that cannot be done on mono canvas. However, the effect is subdued and toned down at this point because the white or ecru threads of the canvas will still show through. The colors will display their true intensity when the stitches are more closely placed, in the final stage.

A SELECTION
OF DESIGNS
FOR CHAIRS

Explained and designed by Maryvonne Dobry

From the period designs on the following pages, you can easily adapt those that you like for use on your own chairs—even if their dimensions are not exactly the same as those of the chairs in the photograph. And you can also readily modify the designs with additional details or an alternate color scheme.

These pages are also a source of ideas for folding screens and firescreens, as well as for cushions, boxes, wastebaskets, and other useful and elegant items that can be enhanced by needlepoint—not to mention motifs that may be used separately for bands on valances or combined with fabrics for countless purposes.

At the beginning of each design, there is a brief description of the features of the chair and its covering that will enable you to identify the style and appropriate motifs and harmonies for your own pieces.

In order to familiarize yourself with the design you have chosen, begin by tracing the diagram given in this book. You will come to understand the details better as you carry out this step. Then, using colored pencils— even if they only approximate the proper hues—mark the principal shades. (Avoid using felt-tipped pens in those bright colors that match absolutely nothing—neither the colors in our photographs nor those of the available yarn.) Always keep this colored diagram at hand, along with the cards of notes that we have advised you to set up. If you also do some "practice exercises," actually stitching details of the motif on separate pieces of canvas, you can keep them in a work folder—unless you decide to make them into pincushions!

Do not forget to refer to the illustration to refresh your memory about some detail that you have forgotten, but do not hesitate, either, to follow some notion of your own—so long as it is not an outright heresy.

For each design, we lay out the steps to follow and provide one or more color schemes.

But you might also consider going back to the section on "Background stitches" (pp. 56-59), to look there for particular effects that would make our models reflect your own taste.

Design 1 Small Louis XIII chair

The polished natural wood of this chair displays the spool turnings on the legs that are hallmarks of this somewhat severe style. The rectangular back, ornamented with wooden moldings, is slightly inclined. The upholstery on the back is recessed, held in place by a narrow molding. The pattern is geometric, worked in "false" Hungarian stitch.

The design can readily be adapted to any other Louis XIII chair: small armchairs with low back and armposts often bearing heads of rams or lions; stools, benches, and—why not—large high-backed chairs. It is worked on penelope. These chevrons will be very lively; you need only find a good color rhythm. In our example, we used, from top to bottom, one gold, one soft green, and one dark green.

After the canvas has been properly bound, you can simplify execution of the stitching if you follow this procedure: turn the canvas (for the back, for instance) so that the right edge faces you horizontally. Mark out reference points to guide yourself, indicating where each new color starts and ends. The color changes are made every 5 stitches and consist of 5 stitches. The pattern shifts are made every 5 rows, for 5 rows. It will be easiest and most convenient to stitch in zigzags, working downward, in cross stitch.

1st row: (in the 1st color) work 5 stitches; *2nd row:* shift 1 stitch to the left; *3rd and 4th rows:* the same; *5th row:* (for one time!) the same. After you have reached the tip of this first pattern, shift the next 4 rows to the right, and the 4 rows after that to the left, and so on. Continue in the same way after each change of color. The stitches must all slant in the same direction, and the points of the chevrons must be identical. For this design, you may do the child's cross stitch *(point de marque),* that is, starting from left to right and returning from right to left to form the cross. Blocking will give your stitches the traditional slant.

Note: This pattern can also be executed in true Hungarian stitch on mono canvas if you mark off the first row (see "Background stitches," no. 8, p. 57).

Be careful when you begin the second piece (for the seat) that you do not change the direction of the canvas. The seat is trapezoidal, as distinguished from the rectangular back. But begin at the right edge, as for the back, to avoid the various pitfalls—in the direction of the stitches, the symmetricalness of the chevrons, the shape of the piece.

To finish off the work, fasten a piece of matching traditional braid or put antiqued nails around the edge.

Color scheme shown

Gold and soft greens	Gold: no. 433 Light gray green: no. 556 Dark green: no. 520	Gray and gray greens	Light gray: no. 389 Medium gray green: no. 594 Dark gray green: no. 340

Other color schemes

		Wood hues	Gold: no. 433 Chestnut: no. 248 Dark chestnut: no. 247
Green blues	Old gold: no. 440 Light green blue: no. 765 Dark green blue: no. 350	Blue and old rose	Periwinkle blue: no. 382 Old rose: no. 260 Deep old rose: no. 245

Design 1   Small Louis XIII chair   Collection Mme. G.-R.   73

Design 2 French Régence

This old needlepoint design of the Régence period (1715-23) has been used on a violin-backed chair made at that time. The geometric motif is outstanding as a design, and its exotic inspiration is evident in its striking color and form.

This design may appear somewhat complicated, but as you break it down analytically and follow the reference points on the accompanying diagrams, you will find that you can reproduce it without difficulty.

You will notice at once that many of the lines can be re-embroidered in silk, as in the piece in the photograph; these lines are indicated on the diagrams by crosshatching.

Beginning at the top:

Central flower
- edges
  - Pale beige: no. 153
  - Brick red: no. 215
- petals
  - Medium beige: no. 136
  - Brick red: no. 215

Central stem of this flower
- Medium taupe: no. 145
- Pale beige: no. 020

Two symmetrical flowers (at right and left)
- leaves
  - Deep blue green: no. 512
  - edge: Wheat: no. 445
  - stems: Gray green: no. 560
- flowers
  - Medium beige: no. 136
  - Light beige: no. 496

(Outline the petals inside of no. 136 with no. 153 and re-embroider in silk.)

Central motif (under the vertical stem)
- Pistils
  - edge: Brick red: no. 215
  - Bronze: no. 445
  - Pale beige: no. 020
- edge
  - Brick red: no. 215
  - Deep blue green: no. 512
- heart
  - Pale beige: no. 153
  - Bronze: no. 445
  - Medium gray: no. 346
- horizontal central ring
  - Soft brown: no. 134
  - Pale beige: no.153

Large motif
- Background: Brick red: no. 215
- upper symmetrical palms:
  - Gray green: no. 560
- edge: Wheat: no. 445
- small motifs: Pale beige: no. 153
- florets
  - edge: Light taupe: no. 492
  - Medium green: no. 546
- stems: Bronze: no. 445

Central flower at bottom
- petals: Pale beige: no. 020 and 153
- heart: Medium green: no. 546
- edge:
  - Bronze: no. 445
  - Pale beige: no. 020

Two symmetrical ascending flowers (at right and left)
- Pale beige: no. 153
- edge:
  - Medium green: no. 546
  - Light taupe: no. 492

Seat for an armchair or side chair
same motif expanded by some details, such as:

Two palms
- Bronze: no. 445
- edge: Gray green: no. 560

Two descending palms (at right and left)
- Deep blue green: no. 512
- Medium beige: no. 136

For elegant small supplementary designs, take your cue from the colors of the designs on the back.

Design 2   French Régence   Collection Brocard   75

Design 3   Armchair à la Reine

Illustration, page 18

The needlepoint upholstery on this truly royal armchair was made especially for it; it is matched to the polychrome paint and the carving on the wood. Although "à la reine" means, of course, "in the style of the queen," it is also used specifically to refer to a straight-backed armchair, as distinguished from a curved-back cabriole.

This motif is a spendid example of the elaborate style of design known as rococo. Strange exotic flowers are set in the midst of foliage within shells that burst from scrolled rocks (rocailles).

As in the paint on the wood, blues dominate and admirably set off the peach of the flowers—a hue that is also a subtle reflection of the gilding. Touches of gold silk edge some of the petals and leaves, and there is a continuous interchange of harmonies from the needlepoint to the wood and from the wood to the needlepoint.

Since the tones have faded somewhat after two hundred years, we have heightened the pinkness in the photograph to brighten the color of the flowers. In reality, the background of the needlepoint has a pure greenish tonality. The foliage in the rocaille scrolls is of two different blue grays, while the foliage of the flowers is a very soft green blue.

The design of the flowers on the back differs slightly from that on the seat. In the former, there is a parrot tulip of a pale peach pink shaded with mauve gray, and the same colors are found in the curious erect flower, in the bellflower, and in the open flower with a blue center. The round flowers are worked in various tones of peach, with gray green or blue green sepals. On the seat, which is, of course, much larger, these same flowers are more important, and the two pearly rocailles inexplicably contain a peach pink corolla.

Another unusual aspect of this covering is that the designs on the two armrests are different. On the left, there is a round flower; on the right, an imaginary stylized carnation.

Color scheme

1. Bellflower
    Parrot tulip
    Erect flower
    - Peach mauve (2 tones): no. 275 and 254
    - Pale peach pink: no. 287
    - Medium taupe: no. 145

2. Open tulip
    (upper left)
    - *heart:* Medium green blue: no. 793
    - Dark peach: no. 269
    - *highlights* (silk):
      Pale peach pink: no. 287

2a. Matching
    foliage
    - Gray green (2 tones): no. 556 and 546
    - *Golden reflections* (silk):
      Light olive green: no. 521

3. Large center
    flower
    - *heart:* Pale peach pink: no. 287
      Light rose beige: no. 257
    - Rose: no. R86
    - Dark peach: no. 269
    - Cinnamon: no. 462

Sepals
    - Gray green (2 tones): no. 522 and 546
    - Dark blue green: no. 516
    - *highlights* (silk): Pale bronze: no. 441

Round
flower
and
its bud
    - Pale peach pink: no. 287
    - Dark peach (2 tones): no. 269 and 266
    - Light rose beige: no. 257
    - Warm brown: no. 174

3a. Foliage for
    large flowers
    - Blue greens (4 tones): no. 350, 330, 334, 306

4. Scrolled
    foliage
    and shells
    - Blue grays (3 tones): no. 381, 380, 314
    - Dark blue gray: no. 334
    - Pale blue green: no. 395

Corollas inside
the scrolled
rocailles
    - Light peach mauve: no. 254
    - Pale peach pink: no. 286
    - Medium peach pink: no. 274

Design 4 Flat cushion *(galette)* for a Louis XV chair

The cane-backed Louis XV-style chair shown on page 83 is a contemporary reproduction. It is made of natural wood with carved moldings and florets. The cambered legs terminate in scrolled feet.

We have provided it with a flat cushion *(galette)* in a needlepoint design of elegant scrolled foliage *(rinceaux)*. In our monochromatic *camaïeu* color scheme—here pink—the foliage stands out against a pale-green background.

For this graceful design, we used a mono canvas no. 12 and 2 strands of yarn in the basketweave stitch. However, since there are always slight differences between one canvas and another, we must caution you to judge for yourself whether you need to use 3 strands for the background. It is important that the canvas be completely covered by your stitches. Not only does that produce a more handsome result, but it is also a guarantee of solidity and durability.

A dark peach to outline or shade, a pale peach pink and a faded peach, underlined by a rust, comprise the *camaïeu*. Observe the choice of this last shade, which is a little brownish. This nuance does not strike a discordant note; rather, contrasting with the peach pinks, it enhances them.

You can adapt this cushion for a Louis XV provincial armchair—it would be an authentic cover. Remember the advice we have given about watching where the wood is placed: in the posts for the back and arms, etc. The scroll design must be positioned inside them, and none of the structural members of the chair should be permitted to encroach on this area.

You can also use this design for handsome cushions to harmonize with your chairs. For these, you can create a "counterbackground" by connecting the scrolled foliage at the left with a fine additional volute (or scroll) that will close the design. Then stitch the background outside the design in a different color, but do not make this contrasting background too dark.

Color scheme		Alternate color scheme	
Background:	Light green: no. 594	Background:	Medium blue green: no. 594 or 350
Scrolled foliage (pink)	Dark peach: no. 269 Pale peach pink: no. 286 Medium peach: no. 281 Rust: no. 274	Scrolled foliage (gold)	Chestnut: no. 248 Caramel: no. 419 Pale yellow: no. 441 Green gold: no. 445

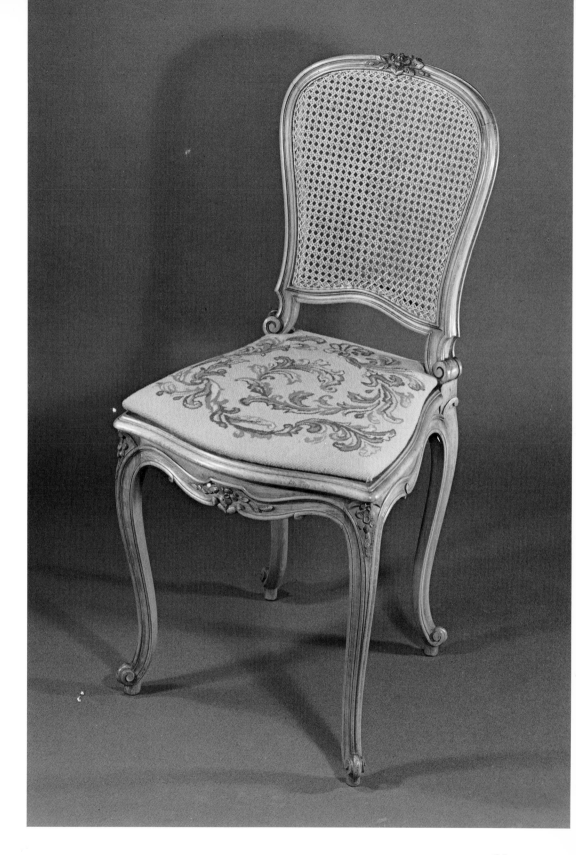

Design 4
Flat cushion
(galette) for
a Louis XV
chair
Collection Mr. G.

Design 5 Louis XV scrollwork and flowers

This piece of antique needlepoint was destined to cover a Louis XV armchair with a traditional design. The central motif is a bouquet of roses, with stylized wild hyacinths, lungworts, and buttercups. It is surrounded by scrolled foliage and garlands of flowers and fruits.

In keeping with eighteenth-century custom, the flowers and the scrolled foliage are worked in wool and the background in silk. The main reason that this needlepoint has lasted for two hundred years is that it was never mounted on a chair, for the silk would never have survived such a long period of use.

The plain piece of linen that served as a support in that era can today fortunately be replaced by the greatly superior mono canvas. For this detailed design, we recommend the finest canvas you are willing to work on. At the lower right of the photograph, there is a small square, which is a sample of the stitch used: the traditional petit-point basketweave.

Although this design may appear dismayingly difficult at first glance, you will find that all the necessary details are given in our diagram, which should facilitate your work. But you can certainly simplify the design if you wish. Keep the general lines, but omit some of the nuances of our extremely sumptuous palette.

Without any change this design can be utilized for a magnificent firescreen.

Color scheme

Background
{ Light beige: no. 492
(Or any other light background that harmonizes with the wood of your chair)

Scrolled foliage
{ *dark edge:* Warm brown: no. 174
middle tone: Medium ocher: no. 411
highlight: Light beige: no. 453

Roses
{ *darkest:* Dark brick red: no. 266
middle tone: Soft rust: no. 248
pink (no longer visible): Pale peach pink: no. 280
small heart: Pale green: no. 542

Leaves
{ *veins:* Dark gray green: no. 516
middle tone: Dark green: no. 506
highlight: Yellow green: no. Y50

Tendrils: Soft brown: no. 134

Buttercups
{ *edges:* Warm brown: no. 174
middle tone: Medium ocher: no. 411
highlight: Light beige: no. 453

Hyacinths: Blue gray (2 tones): no. 380 and 334

Round flowers (Lungworts) lower right
{ *small heart:* Yellow green: no. Y50
small petals: Blue green (2 tones): no. 781 and 330
large petals: Pink taupe (2 tones): no. 132 and 330
edges (no longer visible): Pale peach mauve: no. 870

Buds of the lungworts
{ Pink taupe (2 tones): no. 132 and 133
Pale peach mauve: no. 870

Ribbon around stems: Pale blue green: no. 781

Rosebuds
{ *dark* { Brick red: no. 266
Soft rust: no. 248
sepals { Yellow green: no. Y50
Gray green: no. 560
Medium gray green: no. 546

Stems
{ *dark edge:* Dark brown: no. 144
Soft brown: no. 134
Dark bronze: no. 511

Currants
{ Pink taupe (2 tones): no. 132 and 133
Pale peach mauve: no. 870 (a few stitches)

Other fruits
{ Dark brick red: no. 266
Soft rust: no. 248
Light ocher: no. 441

Design 5   Louis XV scrollwork and flowers   Collection Brocard

Design 6   Louis XV cabriole

This enchanting armchair is of wood painted white, with a soft green accenting the carved roses and florets. Its legs are cambered, and its back has a graceful violin shape.

The needlepoint that covers it is done in basketweave stitch. Its design uses motifs suggested by the carving on the wood: the round and stylized roses and the florets with round and pointed petals are both there. The carnations mark the bouquet as typically Louis XV.

We advise you to do a practice sample (on a separate piece of canvas) of each of the flowers. When you have done them, keep them handy so that you can learn them by heart—and refer to them if you need to in the course of your work.

The tea roses have rosewood-colored hearts and pale-yellow petals with straw-colored highlights and edges of old gold. The hearts of the buttercups are composed of four stitches of rust color and one blue stitch. The starry florets are blue with deep-brown hearts. The carnations are done in three shades of clear pink. The rose leaves have a green reflection (produced by a few stitches worked in a triangle) and are slightly russet, as rose leaves often are. On the small elongated leaves, gray green and yellow green alternate. The leaves of the carnations are contoured by 3 soft greens.

The design for the back of the chair can be adapted very effectively for screens. You can either use the central bouquet surrounded by florets for a firescreen or scatter the individual florets over the panels of a folding screen.

Color scheme

Roses
- *heart:* Light russet: no. 280
- *petals:* Soft brown: no. 462 / Light beige (2 tones): no. 440 and 453
- *edge:* Light taupe: no. 466

Rose leaves
- Dark brown: no. 144
- Soft brown: no. 462
- Pale bronze: no. 441
- Gray green: no. 560
- Dark gray green: no. 516

Buttercups
- *heart:* Rust: no. 274 / Pale blue green: no. 781 (1 stitch)
- *petals:* Soft brown: no. 462 / Ocher: no. 433

Star-shaped florets
- *heart:* Chocolate brown: no. 217
- *petals:* Blue green (2 tones): no. 350 and 395

Elongated leaves
- Dark green: no. 506
- Gray green: no. 560

Carnations
- Medium peach: no. 281
- Pale peach pink: no. 286
- Pale wine: no. 285

Carnation leaves: Gray green (3 tones): no. 516, 546, 556

Background: Pale beige: no. 020

Design 6
Louis XV
cabriole
Design M. Dobry
Collection Mme. P.

Design 7   Roses on a crimson background

Illustration page 23

In this Louis XVI cabriole, with the characteristic concave back, the natural polished wood has been carved into legs with grooved turnings. The rosettes at the corners and the medallion back are also hallmarks of the period. Although this spray of roses is an eighteenth-century design, it actually is typical of the preceding period of Louis XV. However, it is extremely well suited to the shape of the back.

The slender tea roses, with elegantly intertwined stems, have lovely leaves in bronzes and golds. The crimson background emphasizes the delicacy of the design, and its rich color contributes a touch of gaiety to a living room or bedroom.

Study the diagram of each rose carefully. Compare the effect it produces in our photograph. The edges of the petals are luminous, and you can stitch them with a yarn that is almost white. The heart of the flower is taupe, but the petals are a soft brown, edged with a slightly darker brown to make them stand out. Each leaf is modeled with three shades of green browns and a gray-green shadow. The ribs are very dark, and the pointed tip is edged with bronze.

You can make the roses "sing" by re-embroidering the petals with a few stitches of creamy pink silk.

The design is worked in basketweave stitch on a fine canvas of petit-point scale such as mono no. 18. With a bit of skill in using the colors, you can also execute it on a slightly coarser canvas such as mono no. 14.

You can also reduce the number of shades in the leaves.

If you want to cover the panels of a screen with this design, you can use it exactly as it is in this diagram.

Color scheme

Background: Crimson: no. R74

Roses
- heart: Light taupe: no. 466
- petals
  - lights: Pale beige: no. 455
  - middle tones: Light brown: no. 145
  - shadows: Brown: no. 131

Leaves
- Green brown (3 tones): no. 531, 573, and 583
- Medium gray: no. 346
- edges: Bronze: no. 445
- veins: Green beige: no. 521

Stems: Gray green: no. 560

Do not confuse the rosebuds with the tiny leaves.

Design 8   Louis XVI medallion-back armchair

With its frame of wood painted white, its turned and fluted legs, rosettes at the corners of the seat, oval concave back with decorative molding—this armchair, like the preceding one, is very typical of the period of Louis XVI. The design of the needlepoint that covers it is traditional: a bouquet of roses, an arabesque of delicate foliage, a garland of roses and charming tasseled bowknots.

Only a few colors: two rosy reds for the flowers and the bowknots, two greens for the leaves and the foliage. This design is very restrained; it is in essence a double set of monochromes. Its elegance depends entirely on the choice of the two pairs of colors.

The background here is solid. However, the design allows you to create a slightly darker counterbackground; the central bouquet will then seem to be illuminated. It will be easy to confine the stitching of the counterbackground at the outer limits of the garland. With the garland standing out against the darker background at the edges and against the lighter ground in the center, the pink tones will sing quite differently. Another possibility for the counterbackground would be to extend it to cover all the background behind the garland. This will further shrink and illuminate the light background behind the bouquet.

The flowers here are stylized, lightly modeled by two tones of faded rose; two tones of antique green give depth to the leaves. The dainty foliage in arabesques has an even simpler color scheme: the stems are dark, the small leaves light. We used a dark blue green and a pale, slightly beige green. A brownish red and a rose set the bowknots and their tassels into relief. The cast of the background tones must reflect the tone of the lacquer on the wood and at the same time set off the colors of the design. This was very skillfully achieved here.

For the armrests, take a flower and a bud from the bottom of the bouquet. The armrests should be designed as mirror images, with the reversed designs facing each other. Usually, the armrests should be worked in the darkest color of the background, if there are two of them.

No change is necessary to use the motif on this medallion back for a firescreen or for the panels of a folding screen. Add a simple darker band all around to serve as a frame and to balance the entire piece.

If you omit the central motif (and keep only the wreath of roses, bowknots, and foliage, on a solid background), you will discover a remarkably graceful design that would in itself be perfect for a firescreen. Alternatively, this same wreath could be very much enlarged for the proportions of a folding screen, while at the same time the central bouquet, left in its original size in the center, would stand more apart in an atmosphere of great airiness. Finally, you can enlarge the bouquet alone and work it on a solid background. You need only frame it with a band of one of the pairs of monochromes you used in the motif.

Color scheme

Background:	Pale beige: no. 496	Roses and bowknots	Dark wine: no. 205 / Deep old rose: no. 245
Leaves	Forest green: no. 506 / Medium yellow green: no. 573	Counterbackground:	Pale beige: no. 466

94

Design 8
Louis XVI
medallion-back
armchair
Collection M. J.

Designs 9 and 10   Louis XVI chairs with "Chinese birds"

These charming, dainty lyre-backed chairs, in painted wood, are upholstered in needlepoint inspired by Chinese porcelain.

The design was created especially for them and was conceived as a mirror image, as it should be for two chairs that are seen, for the most part, in a single glance. And notice the choice of the braid for the border which exactly echoes the pearled edges of the lyres.

The work is extremely delicate, perfectly in keeping with the stylizations we find on needlepoint of this period. (It was in the eighteenth century, in fact, that Chinese art was "discovered" by Europe.) A tiny mountain, a rock, the classic twisted bough on which a bird is poised, and in the sky a flight of butterflies or birds in silhouette.

We suggest two different color schemes for these chairs, but both are in the same spirit. In our photograph you will recognize the ambience that you must convey in your own needlework.

Each of the designs could be used intact for an elegant firescreen. With a graceful frame (stitched on the edge of the needlepoint itself), and the color of the sky rendered more natural by a tint that is barely blue—or barely green—these designs would lend themselves also to wall hangings.

The bird in design 9 is perched on a Chinese lantern vine. Its large leaves are a warm green, given depth by gilded bronze and dark veins. The fruits are orange, with pale brick highlights and brown veins.

Color scheme for no. 9

Bird	Pink taupe: no. 133 Dark gray blue: no. 380 Light gray: no. 164 Light russet: no. 280	Bough	Dark olive green: no. 540 Bronze: no. 433
		Butterflies	Brick red: no. 225 Light green: no. 542
Leaves	Medium yellow green: no. 573 Dark olive green: no. 540 Bronze: no. 433	Fruits (Lanterns)	Orange: no. 426 Pale brick red: no. 278 Soft brown: no. 145

The pale-blue parakeet of design 10 is perched on a vine full of autumn leaves. A little bush at one side and a patch of strange leaves on the other contrast with the foreground, where pale violet shadows play over a pool of water and soft turf.

Treat this foreground like a print, like a mosaic of water-colors.

Color scheme for no. 10

Bird	Pale blue green: no. 781 Pale blue: no. 756 Dark gray blue: no. 380	Bough	Soft brown (2 tones): no. 462 and 145 Caramel: no. 419 Brown: no. 154		
Autumn leaves	Light russet: no. 280 Gray green: no. 560 Medium gray green: no. 546 Bronze: no. 433 Yellow gold: no. 440	Strange leaves	Light green: no. 591 Olive green: no. 505	Color scheme for both foregrounds	Light green: no. 542 Medium yellow green: no. 573 Pale violet: no. 127 Gray green: no. 556 With touches of light and shade
		Bush	Gray green (2 tones): no. 556 and 522 Soft brown: no. 145		

Designs 9 and 10 in the same style as designs 9 and 10.
Design M. Dobry   Collection Mr. G.

Louis XVI chairs with "Chinese birds"

Design 11 Louis XVI monochromatic *camaïeu*

Here is an authentic piece of needlepoint dating from the Louis XVI period that is suitable for an armchair with a rectangular back or one with a basket-handle back.

It is a design of elegant simplicity consisting of a basket of flowers inside a medallion, surrounded by intertwined flowering branches. Each element is highly stylized.

Even in this black and white photograph, you can readily distinguish four different shades. Since this is a *camaïeu,* the palette is monochromatic, here composed of blues: a deep blue, a medium blue, a slightly grayish blue, and one that is almost white. A background of pale ocher completes this extremely handsome color scheme.

For a firescreen or a folding screen, you can take just the central motif of the design: the medallion with its flower basket held by the bowknot of ribbon from which small flowering branches escape.

For a folding screen, you might frame your design with a triple border that has the same color combination and appearance as the medallion that surrounds the basket.

You can easily create a contrasting counterbackground bounded by the outside of the garland. Choose a color for the counterbackground that is a shade darker than that of the central background, remaining, of course, in the same family.

If you are using only the central motif, but adding a counterbackground, keep the background itself very luminous. Choose a brighter tone for the counterbackground so that the flowering branches escaping from the medallion will stand out against it.

And remember that you can change the effect of the counterbackground by using one of the fancy stitches in the section on backgrounds (pp. 56-59). All this can be achieved with just one color.

Another suggestion: for an oblong cushion, enlarge only the central motif at the bottom of the garland—the three flowers and their buds, the jagged leaves, and the two small flowering branches above. You will have a strikingly pure and restrained design.

Color scheme in blue		Color scheme in pink	
Background:	Light ocher: no. 441	Background	*delicate blue:* Periwinkle: no. 392
Motif	*dark:* Dark blue gray: no. 334 *medium:* Gray blue: no. 389 *barely blue:* Pale blue green: no. 556 *almost white:* Pale blue: no. 781	Motif	*dark:* Mauve pink: no. 223 *medium:* Medium mauve pink: no. 250 *slightly faded:* Light peach mauve: no. 254 *almost white:* Pale pink: no. 265

Design 11 Louis XVI monochromatic *camaïeu*   Collection Brocard

Design 12   Louis XVI monochromatic *camaïeu*

This painted canvas, with its symmetrical design of stylized round flowers, is thoroughly in the spirit of the period of Louis XVI. An armful of flowers caught by a ribbon bowknot in the center is depicted with the clarity that *camaïeu* permits. On the design for the back, there is the interesting addition of two facing birds.

Study the flowers carefully: a bold, dark rim, a center with four light-russet-colored stamens, a middle tone of soft pink. Work a practice piece (which will become your model) to learn how to form the curves of each petal properly; make certain that the points between them are clearly defined. Although the flowers are symmetrical, they are not turned in the same way; there are three different positions. Study them.

Also practice making the pink florets with the russet centers; they require particular observation. Even though they are very small, they must retain—and convey—the shape of a flower.

The beaks and the feet of the stylized birds also demand careful execution with just a few well-placed stitches. Alternate the pinks of the leaves so that they will stand out a little against each other. And in working the bowknots, be sure to keep them graceful.

This design takes its balance from the stems of the flowers, which form elegant arabesques, even on the seat, which is very large in comparison with the small back. For the stems, we used a brick with a chestnut tinge.

For the armrests, pick one round flower, and surround it with two three-lobed leaves set diagonally on the top and bottom, with a floret and a few small leaves alongside.

We suggest a pink color scheme; if your chair is lacquered in gray with a bluish tinge or with a slightly greenish cast, make the background a creamy pink. If the lacquer is whitish beige, use an off white or very, very pale green, which will provide contrast. Another extremely distinguished color scheme consists of a group of blue grays against a pale-pink background. A more traditional color scheme uses several blues against a gold background.

The proportions of the back of this armchair lend themselves particularly well to a firescreen.

Color scheme in pink		Color scheme in blue		Color scheme in green	
Background:	Pale peach pink: no. 287	Background:	Peach pink: no. 286	Background:	Light ocher: no. 441
Motif	Medium peach: no. 281 Russet (darker): no. 274 Russet (lighter): no. 280 Peach pink: no. 286 Chestnut: no. 154	Motif	Indigo blue: no. 350 Dark blue gray: no. 334 Medium blue green: no. 594 Pale blue green: no. 556 Pale blue green (lighter): no. 781	Motif	Gray green: no. 556 Gray green (darker): no. 560 Light green: no. 594 Green brown: no. 521 Light green (paler): no. 590

Design 12 Louis XVI monochromatic *camaïeu*   Canvas painted by M. Dobry

Design 13 Louis XVI cabriole

The legs of this small Louis XVI armchair in polished wood are turned and fluted, with rosettes at the corners. It has a basket-handle back. It is complemented by the needlepoint covering in the classic design of vertical stripes with little roses mentioned on page 25.

We advise you to mark your canvas roughly before beginning to work. Then you can proceed to do the repeat design with no fear of error.

Study the enlarged detail on page 112, in which you can distinguish each stitch. The bands of stripes are 19 stitches wide; the little roses are worked inside a band 18 stitches wide. Lay out your design on the canvas so that there will be a band of roses running down the center of the back and the center of the seat.

Stitch the stripes vertically, working downward. They consist of four colors, forming narrower stripes inside the bands. The 19 stitches are divided as follows: 2 chestnut stitches, 3 yellow, 3 gray, 3 blue, and—completing the symmetry—3 gray, 3 yellow, and 2 chestnut.

The little roses are worked within a band with a gray-beige background that is 18 stitches wide. Between the outer edge of each leaf and the closest stripe, there are 3 background stitches. The flower is 13 stitches high. Work the little roses first and fill in the background afterward. Be careful to avoid getting lumps at the beginning and end of each thread as you change color.

Begin with the green heart. In the *1st row,* 3 stitches; in the *2nd row,* 5 stitches; in the *3rd row,* 3 stitches. Then go to the pale pink, working around the heart. Begin, for example, at the right: *1st row:* 1 stitch, next to the heart; *2nd row:* 1 stitch; *3rd row:* 4 stitches; *4th row:* 6 stitches; *5th row:* 5 stitches. Now go back up to the *3rd row* (to the left of the heart): 2 stitches, then to the *2nd row* (also to the left): 1 stitch; and finally to the *1st row:* 1 stitch.

With the dark pink, go back to the right under the pale pink and finish at the left.

Complete the design with the little leaves and the stem, counting stitches carefully.

Color scheme

Stripes	Chestnut: no. 174 Yellow: no. 445 Gray: no. 164 Blue: no. 346	

Roses	*heart:*	Light green gray: no. 556
	petals:	Old rose (pale): no. 260
		Old rose (dark): no. 207
	leaves:	Dark gray green: no. 522

Taupe background:	Taupe: no. 140

You can use another color combination for the band of stripes, but retain the suggested colors for the little roses, which will harmonize with everything.

Design 13   Louis XVI cabriole   Collection Mme. P.-M.

Design 13
Louis XVI
cabriole

Design 14　Empire rosette

Illustration page 26

Turn back to page 26 to look at the photograph of the small Empire chair upholstered in needlepoint. The design has a central rosette on a two-tone counted-stitch background, and the frame has truncated corners crowned with palmettes. The seat is made with a vertical band *(plate-bande)* drawn down over the sides all around; this is worked in the background stitch. The rosette, the frame, the palmettes, and the stars are in bronze on a background of Empire green.

Our diagram permits you to adapt this very classic design for either a period armchair or a period footstool. You can enlarge the starry background as much as you want, or extend the frame.

You might wish to transpose this design to Gobelin stitch, which is extremely well suited to Empire pieces. In that case, draw the motifs carefully and mark off the background, which you will work later in a special background stitch.

You might also turn back to the section on "Period bands" (pp. 62-63) and look at the design of bees (C), done in Gobelin stitch. You can use our rosette design as a basis and—if you need a wide band to edge it—you can insert these traditional Empire bees, which would be very appropriate. Or you could eliminate the frame with palmettes and keep only the center rosette, and then at regular intervals, place the bees over the entire background, instead of the stars. They would be equally effective on a green or a garnet background.

For a firescreen, adapt this design to the desired dimensions without changing anything, or follow one of the preceding suggestions.

Color scheme

Background:　　Olive green: no. 505

Motif　　　　{ Light rust: no. 433
　　　　　　　　Caramel: no. 419
　　　　　　　　Pale bronze: no. 441

Design 15   Small romantic landscape

Illustration page 117

This antique tapestry, taken from a small chair, is a typically romantic fantasy.

In this piece, the needlepoint was worked so that the fabric support was permitted to show through. The design was executed in wool; there was certainly once a graceful braid edging that formed a boundary for the counterbackground, worked in silk.

Study the photograph. Even though it is not in color, you can see the different shades within the monochromatic palette. It goes from pale beige to an almost black brown, moving through several taupe and brown shades that we list below.

The motif is worked in half-cross stitch, slanting in the wrong direction; undoubtedly, the man or woman who executed it was lefthanded.

The counter background is done in cross stitch. The dye of the blue silk has not held, which often happened with the dyes of that period; the various discolorations undoubtedly indicate that there were several different dye lots. The blue was a slightly turquoise sky blue, and it harmonized delicately with the brown and beige tones of the monochrome.

Although the support on which it was stitched was very fine, one worked on it as on a canvas, counting the threads to achieve perfectly even stitches. Here each half-cross stitch covered 2 vertical threads and 2 horizontal.

In this particular case, it would be extremely unwise to try to draw on the fabric with a felt-tipped pen. Instead, use gray carbon paper with washable ink (the kind used to transfer embroidery and crewel designs). Draw your design to the desired scale, and then trace it lightly. If your stitches cover the drawing completely, do nothing more. If not, wash the needlepoint and lay it flat to dry, well stretched, before working the counterbackground or the border.

From this charming design, would you not gladly make a picture or ornamental cushion? You can see that a great many possibilities are offered by this kind of picture, and you find inspiration from many sources.

Color scheme

Trees
- *shadow:* Dark brown: no. 115
- *middle tone:* Soft brown: no. 462
- *light:* Light taupe: no. 492

Ground
- *shadow:* Taupe (2 tones): no. 466 and 145
- *light:* Pale beige (2 tones): no. 105 and 455

Shrubbery
- *dark shadow:* Dark brown: no. 115
- *shadow:* Taupe (2 tones): no. 466 and 145
- *soft light:* Pale beige: no. 455

Buildings
- *dark shadows:* Dark brown: no. 115
- *shadow:* Taupe (2 tones): no. 466 and 145
- *light* { Pale beige: no. 455 / Light taupe: no. 492

Design 15

116

Design 15   Small romantic landscape   Collection Brocard

Designs 16 and 17   Napoleon III Chinese silhouettes

These pieces were originally intended for the seats of graceful little Napoleon III chairs, in black wood, with small columns forming the backs. Since the part attached to the frame was damaged, we cut it off and stitched on an edging of woolen cording of the same color as the background to create these charming seat pads. This is an example of how you can make fresh, delightful use of old needlepoint that is no longer intact. Because the design was still in sufficiently good condition, it was possible to reuse these two pieces of needlepoint as flat cushions *(galettes)* by giving them a backing of the same red. If one added a solid band all around, even with larger stitches, they could also be fastened directly onto chairs again.

You can omit the garlands and enlarge only the little Chinese scenes to cover a seat completely, or to make captivating cushions.

If you want to make the designs *round,* modify the garlands by using only the motifs of the upper corners. To make them *square,* use only the motifs of the lower corners.

With two garlands, you can make bands for a piano keyboard cover and bell pulls.

If you trace two corners face to face, you will have a complete motif. Notice how many different uses you can derive from these delightful examples of *chinoiserie.*

Our photograph makes the diagonal stitches stand out. The yarn used originally to work the backgrounds certainly did not come from the same dye lot. The black has faded also, but more evenly.

A very fine mono canvas was used here, and you may not have the patience to embark on such a taxing project. We suggest that you work the black motif in petit point (why not?) on penelope canvas, which will permit you to stitch the backgrounds in a very much larger basketweave.

For this design, we advise you to depart from customary practice and use—along with the tomato red—a truly *black* yarn.

Gobelin stitch, on a penelope canvas turned sideways (p. 49) would lend itself very well also to these designs.

Designs 16 and 17　　Napoleon III Chinese silhouettes　　Collection M. D.

Design 18   Louis XIII for modern chairs

This painted canvas shows a design typical of the Louis XIII period, consisting of exotic flowers and fruits. The only departure from the ancient model is that we have restored the original vivacity of the colors. It is suitable for chairs of imposing size.

The patina of time has made us forget that originally these large chairs were upholstered with vivid patterns in brilliant colors. In the vast halls, themselves somber and forbidding, they furnished a touch of life and warmth. We suggest that you use this design for modern chairs. Their geometric, spare lines are related to the sober contours of this traditional style. While in days gone by they were suffused in shadows, these brightly colored pieces will stand out gaily in the contemporary ambience, which is sometimes somewhat cold.

This canvas is prepared to be worked in Gobelin stitch, which suits this design very well. Use a penelope canvas turned sideways (p. 49).

Color scheme

Pinks	Peach mauve (3 tones): no. 254, 275, and 205 Lilac pink: no. 137
Ochers and browns	Yellow green: no. Y50 Light beige: no. 453 Light rust: no. 433 Caramel: no. 419 Chestnut: no. 248 Light gold: no. 441
Reds	Brick red (2 tones): no. 269 and 266 Peach beige: no. 257 Dark wine: no. 201
Greens	Medium gray green: no. 546 Light green: no. 591 Dark olive green: no. 540 Dark green: no. 520
Blues:	Blue green (3 tones): no. 342, 367, and 340
Greige	Pale greige: no. 132 or Medium greige: no. 138 for the background

This color combination is neither very dazzling nor very subdued. Of course, you can modify it according to your taste, simplifying or complicating the choice of shades. In any event, the more colors you use in the needlepoint, the better it will harmonize with different settings.

Design 18   Louis XIII for modern chairs   Canvas painted by M. Dobry

Pillows

Four period pillows surround a modern example with a geometric design worked in cross stitch. The large exotic flower with the traditional greenery is in basketweave. The Louis XIII motif in monochromatic tones of green on a gold background is worked in cross stitch. The pink parakeet is done in Gobelin stitch, as are the three Louis XV birds, executed with remarkable delicacy. Perhaps these pieces will serve to inspire you to create your own pillow designs.

Reproductions

Here is an example of the adaptation to canvas, in Gobelin stitch, of an old tapestry design from the Gobelins manufactury.

The back of this large Louis XV provincial armchair is covered in authentic tapestry; the seat is covered in needlepoint. The design was copied exactly; pains were taken to reproduce the age-worn colors, and an attempt was even made to imitate some effects of wear.

While certain devotees seek to rediscover the original colors, which are astonishingly preserved from the effects of light on the wrong side of tapestries, others prefer, like us in the case of this chair, to preserve the harmony created by the patina of time.

The foliage that frames the parakeet has taken on warm ocher tones. The greens have become bluish, the brown of the tree and of the two or three leaves seen against the light produce a striking relief effect. The large exotic flowers at the front of the seat have the same colors as the parakeet. The effect as a whole is captivating and it works particularly well with the polished natural wood. It is a faithful reproduction, very comfortable in all kinds of settings.

First of all, reproduce the major outlines of the design—trace them from your used canvas or tapestry on glassine or tracing paper. Choose the principal colors, observing how they are divided up on your original. You will easily understand the general idea of the color scheme. The same colors must be continued from one motif to another, blending and joining at the same time. Remember the principle of shading colors in multiples of three: one dark, one light, and one middle tone, divided (and redivided if you want) into three. Always keep at hand a piece of the original tapestry in sufficiently good condition so that you can compare it to your work and check your color choices as you go along.

Louis XV
provincial
armchair
Collection M. D.

Photographic credits

Collection Brocard (Jean-Claude Carel): p. 75 — Studio Lourmel, Paris: pp. 29, 35, 73, 83, 89, 99, 125, 127 — Philippe R. Doumic, Paris: pp. 23, 33, 56, 58, 60, 61, 63, 85, 95, 103, 107, 111, 112, 117, 119, 123 — Cliché Plaisir de France, (Claude Basnier): Frontispiece.

All the other illustrations are from the book *Le Siège français,* by Madeleine Jarry.

This book was printed in the month of June, 1976, on the presses of the Imprimerie Fragnière S.A., Fribourg.— Photoengraving: Newgrafart S.A., Fribourg. — Binding: H. and J. Schumacher S.A., Schmitten-Berne. — Production: Barbara Perroud. Manufacture: Franz Stadelmann. Artistic adviser: Léon Larfillon.

Printed in Switzerland.

Jarry.
Period needlepoint for
antique furniture.

DATE DUE